Dropshipping

Start Your Own E-Commerce Business on Shopify, Amazon, or E-Bay and Make Money Online from Home with this comprehensive guide for beginners (2022 Guide for Beginners)

Jewel Garza

Content List

INTRODUCTION

To dropship or not to dropship is the question you must answer. This is the question that any entrepreneur asks himself or herself when deciding to start a dropshipping business. Many people will immediately advise you to avoid this business model because it is a scam and you will never make any money.

You are the captain of your own ship, and you must make an informed decision to launch your company. This is why, as a beginner, this book will walk you through the basics step by step, allowing you to create your business calmly and logically. Your goal is success, which you will achieve with the guidance provided and by getting off to a good start, despite the doomsday predictions of the naysayers who give unwelcome bad advice.

So let's get started with everything you need to know and understand, as well as how to set up your dropshipping business with the least amount of fuss and bother.

CHAPTER 1

START FROM THE BEGINNING

Starting off on the right foot and answering all of the important questions is critical to your success. Getting it right the first time is far easier than trying to go back and fix mistakes you made because you were impatient or tried to take shortcuts.

What Exactly Is Dropshipping?

Dropshipping is a type of e-commerce business model.

Unlike traditional e-commerce, you do not physically handle the products you sell, nor do you stockpile the products that you offer for sale. You create your online e-commerce store using your own website or a platform like Shopify, Amazon, or eBay.

You provide specific products to your clients that are available from reputable wholesale suppliers and manufacturers who specialize in the products in your chosen niche. The chain reaction begins when your client places an order with you.

You, in turn, make a purchase order with your supplier. Your supplier charges you for the product at the agreed-upon price and then ships it directly to your client.

Depending on your niche products, your suppliers could be located anywhere on the planet. There are no restrictions on where your suppliers are located; this works for sensitive products as well as shortening the timeframe from manufacture to delivery to client because inventory is not sitting on a shelf in the hopes of being sold before the expiry date.

When you decide to start a business using the dropshipping business model, it changes the way you do business and adds enormous flexibility to your company's daily operations.

It's Critical to Have the Right Mindset

To make your dropshipping business a success, you must cultivate a strong entrepreneurial mindset from the beginning. You can't start your own business if you're apathetic and couldn't care less. You are setting yourself up for failure if you do so. You must be hungry for success and enter this venture with a can-do attitude and determination.

Commitment

You must fully commit to this business venture and make use of all available resources. The best part is that you can fully commit to starting your dropshipping business even if you have another job; you don't have to give up one for the other. You can juggle how you handle client inquiries and orders around your other job if you are dedicated. This allows you to start your company and allow it to grow until you are ready to make the full transition to running your company. If you fully commit from the start, you will reap the benefits of a smoothly running business that requires less time to maintain once it gains traction.

Perseverance

We all live in an instant-gratification world, where we expect instant gratification for everything from food and entertainment to finances and anything we want to buy. We've grown accustomed to obtaining anything with the click of a mouse or the touch of a button. Unfortunately, this has instilled in many people a spoiled and petulant attitude that does not foster strong character, commitment, and perseverance.

Your perseverance is essential to your success. There are numerous quotes and sayings about perseverance, not giving up and trying again if you don't succeed the first time. There is a reason for these sayings; they mean that you are not the first person to face difficulties or problems, and those sayings were coined by people who persevered, kept going, and tried until they found exactly what worked for them. Perseverance leads to determination, which leads to a greater commitment to succeed, which is exactly what you need to start your own dropshipping business. Even if things don't fall into place right away, you just keep going until each aspect of your business falls neatly into place one by one.

There is no quick fix attitude.

When it comes to starting your own business, there are no quick fixes. Attempting to skip necessary steps in order to save time and effort will doom this venture to failure. Do not be tempted by get-rich-quick schemes that promise a million dollar income with no effort; such schemes do not exist. Get rid of any quick fix mentality; it will only lead to you wasting money and skipping necessary steps during the startup phase of your business, which will be costly to correct later on. Do things correctly from the start and build your dropshipping business on a solid foundation that will be able to withstand setbacks and other problems as time passes.

Time and energy should be invested.

The phrase "blood, sweat, and tears" may sound overly dramatic, but you must invest your time and energy to make your dropshipping business a success. People far too often want to pour large sums of money into a business venture; there is no need to do so. Dropshipping allows you to own your own business with little capital by investing yourself and using your energy to get it off the ground.

This type of investment has numerous advantages that will benefit you in the long run as your business grows.

- As you gain firsthand experience of how each aspect of your business operates, your skills and knowledge will grow with it.
- Money cannot buy the skills you will gain from running your own business. When you begin to expand, you will understand how each section of the

company operates, which is necessary for managing the other people you will hire.

- You will learn about your customers, how they think, and what they want. Markets are constantly changing, and as a hands-on member of the company's management team, you will learn about market trends in order to keep your customers satisfied. This will enable you to make decisions about which suppliers to use and marketing strategies for your website to entice potential customers to use your services.

- When you are intimately involved in the day-to-day operations of your company, you learn what to spend money on that is critical to the company's success. Your mindset shifts, and your priorities shift away from non-essentials that may appear nice or gadgets that you can easily live without.

Concentrate on Solutions, Not Problems

We frequently become so engrossed in the details of a problem that we lose sight of the bigger picture. Instead of thinking, "I have a problem, I don't know what to do," flip your mindset and start with, "I have to find a solution to this problem."

Train your mind to see things from a solution perspective rather than a problem perspective. Instead of worrying, explore all of your options for finding solutions. The internet literally puts knowledge at your fingertips. If you're having trouble with a supplier, start looking for other options. Discover what's available on Amazon, eBay, and Shopify and how you can use these platforms to your advantage to solve the problem you're having. There are numerous dropshipping blogs where people share information and advice on how they solved their problems. The solutions are available; you simply need to invest some time in researching the best options that meet your requirements.

Mistakes should be viewed as a learning opportunity rather than a failure.

Mistakes are not the end of the world; no one on the planet can claim to have never made a mistake in their lives. Mistakes occur in all types of businesses. However, how you handle the mistake and what you do about it makes a significant difference.

A mistake does not imply that you are a complete failure and should close down your new dropshipping business. Every mistake provides an opportunity to learn. You will learn how to solve problems and avoid making the same mistakes in the future.

Mistakes teach you important lessons in customer service. You learn how to admit mistakes and how to appease irate customers without losing them. Every customer service situation you handle improves your customer service skills and will help you in the future.

A supplier error allows you to hone your skills in cooperation and negotiation, which benefits both your business and the business of your supplier.

CHAPTER 2

WHY SHOULD YOU START A DROPSHIPPING BUSINESS?

Is Your Time and Effort Really Worth It?

Yes, it is a resounding yes. You will not get a stress-free way to generate income if you start any type of business. You will need to work hard and be dedicated to your business. You can expect the outcome to clearly demonstrate the amount of effort and time you are willing to put into this.

The reality that all businesses must face today is that we live in a world that has changed dramatically over the last few decades. Strategies that worked 30 years ago are now out of date, and if you want to be competitive and successful, you must adapt and grow to keep up with how technological advances have influenced how people shop. People no longer want to go to stores and be limited to what is available in that particular store. Everyone has time constraints and wants to get as much done as possible in a day, so it is far more convenient to use a smartphone or laptop to do their shopping.

E-commerce has taken over the world, and the dropshipping business model fits in well as global markets become more competitive. People now prefer to shop online and have their purchases delivered directly to them, so the retail behemoths of a few decades ago are floundering. This is understandable given the introduction of e-commerce to global shopping.

This chart, provided by Business Insider and based on data from their own company, depicts the bleak reality that traditional retailers face. The graph clearly demonstrates why starting your own dropshipping business is worth your time and effort.

(2018, Business Insider)

CHAPTER 3

DROPSHIPPING BUSINESS MODEL BENEFITS

A Dropshipping is fundamentally different from traditional retail outlets in that you do not operate from a physical business location, which drastically alters how you conduct business. Dropshipping differs from traditional e-commerce in that these businesses buy inventory and ship orders to customers from that inventory.

Dropshipping has a plethora of advantages that are unique to the dropshipping business model.

Lower Capital Invested

Yes, some capital is required to start a business. The big difference is that you don't need a lot of money to get started with your dropshipping business. You only need some cash as a safety net while you work on getting your company up and running. All businesses have minor operating expenses, and you should be aware that you should budget for web hosting costs as well as any fees associated with using dropshipping platforms. It's a good idea to keep some cash on hand for unexpected expenses. Keeping this in mind will reduce stress and allow you to concentrate on getting your business off the ground.

Simple to Get Started

Because you do not physically transport stock, you do not require a warehouse to store inventory. This means you don't have any warehouse-related expenses, such as property rental or warehouse equipment. This also eliminates all of the complications that come with running a warehouse. There are no wasted hours spent reordering stock and keeping strict inventory records.

You are not in charge of packing, labelling, or shipping the products you sell, nor are you in charge of inbound product shipments or returns. This makes it far easier to launch your business and eliminates the logistical nightmare of packaging and shipping.

Overheads

Overheads are a nightmare that businesses face on a daily basis. Because you can start and run your business from home, the dropshipping business model eliminates the majority of overhead expenses. It is natural for your overhead expenses to rise as your business expands, but your costs will always be significantly lower than those of a traditional retail outlet.

Location

Having a dropshipping business gives you the most flexibility in terms of location, as you can run it from anywhere you have internet access. You don't need fancy and expensive offices to impress potential customers; all you need is a laptop and internet, which is ideal because you can conduct business whether you're sitting at a desk at home or travelling.

The Global Market

You have access to markets all over the world when you use e-commerce and the dropshipping business model; you are not limited to local products in your country. Dropshipping is possible from any supplier or manufacturer in the world. Customers find this very appealing because they have a much wider range to choose from than would be possible from any retailer in their area.

This graph depicts the enormous global popularity of e-commerce. You can easily access global markets for your dropshipping business by using online retail platforms.

(MGR Consulting Group)

Product Availability in Your Niche Is Extensive

Because only certain suppliers may carry the products that you require, niche products can often be very restrictive in terms of what products you can add to your e-commerce business. If you were only limited to local markets, this would cause major issues, limit your business's growth, and have a negative impact on your profit margin. Access to global markets is a game changer for niche products, making this a top benefit for all niche product sellers.

Significantly Lower Risk Factors

Dropshipping, as opposed to the more traditional e-commerce business model, has a significant advantage in lowering the risks of monetary loss to the dropshipping seller because you do not run the risk of not being able to sell the inventory you have already paid for. If you have a slow period and do not make a sale, the only monetary loss is the potential profit from a sale.

Another risk-reducing factor is that you only place the order with your supplier after your customer has placed and paid for an order with you. When you contact your supplier, you use the money that has already been paid to you rather than your own money, so you do not have to always ensure that you have extra funds when you place an order with your supplier.

A win-win situation for both the supplier and the dropshipping business

Suppliers and manufacturers are eager to collaborate with dropshipping companies because the more people who sell their products, the greater their overall profits. Suppliers are willing to negotiate a lower or wholesale price with dropshipping companies, even if the dropshipping companies do not purchase his products in bulk.

Their enthusiasm stems from the fact that they gain greater exposure for their products while incurring no marketing costs, as well as having more time to produce their goods. Suppliers are well aware that developing a positive relationship with the dropshipping company ensures that the company will return to them to purchase more products at a reasonable price.

With a more productive supplier and a loyal dropshipping company that keeps a steady flow of orders coming in, this is a win-win situation for everyone, resulting in increased profit for both the supplier and the dropshipping business.

Making Use of Online Retail Platforms

Using online retail platforms is critical to the success of your dropshipping business. In later chapters, we will go over the online retail platforms in greater detail, but for now, we will look at the general benefits.

Unrestricted Customer Exposure

Every online store wants to reach as many potential customers as possible. When you join the online retail platforms, you instantly gain access to virtually unlimited customers without having to spend a fortune on marketing.

A Wide Range of Products in Your Niche to Choose From

Another significant advantage of using online retail platforms is the vast array of products available that fall within your niche; you can pick and choose what you believe is best for you, and if you discover that a particular product is not selling well, you can easily switch to another product available on the platform. Experimenting with which products sell the best is a low-cost venture when you use retail platforms because you don't lose money on unsold inventory. Keeping track of your selling trends allows you to switch and change quickly in order to stay on top of your game.

A plethora of unfilled niches

Amazon, Shopify, and eBay always have a large number of vacant niches for you to explore, which is a fantastic opportunity for you to expand your business into more than one niche. The retail platforms do the legwork, and your company benefits without you having to spend hours and hours researching new opportunities.

Scaling

What is scaling in the context of a dropshipping business, and how does it work? This is one of the most frequently asked questions by entrepreneurs starting their own dropshipping business.

Growing and expanding your dropshipping business is what scaling up entails. Scaling this business model is far easier than scaling a traditional e-commerce business because the traditional business model requires significantly more work; the more orders received, the more work is involved.

The process is different for a dropshipping business. Your dropshipping suppliers handle the majority of the work generated to process more orders, making the growing process easier for you and eliminating the majority of the growing pains that other companies face.

CHAPTER 4

BE AWARE OF DRAWBACKS

All business models have advantages and disadvantages, the dropshipping model is no exception. This is not to say that it is a bad business model; rather, you should be aware of the drawbacks that are unique to dropshipping. You make allowances for the disadvantages, try to avoid them as much as possible, and find solutions to problems wherever possible. Faced with setbacks, your business does not have to fail; you can overcome many setbacks by planning ahead of time and putting backup solutions in place.

The Margin Is Narrow

The low margins in their chosen niche turn off many people. People want to see higher profits and faster growth in their businesses. If you are willing to start small, persevere, and learn everything there is to know about running a dropshipping business in the highly competitive field of e-commerce, you will grow steadily and reap the benefits of your efforts.

Market Place Competition

E-commerce is highly competitive, with sellers undercutting one another in order to make more money faster. Dropshipping businesses are simple to establish with a small cash investment, making them a highly competitive business model. The best way to deal with this is to start your business correctly, provide quality service to your customers, and use all available resources to build a good business reputation.

Inventory and Product Fulfillment Issues

As a dropshipping business model, you do not have control over your inventory and are unable to track the flow of stock.

You rely on suppliers and wholesalers who also serve many other merchants. This can lead to problems with products being out of stock at the time you place your order.

Your suppliers are in charge of product fulfilment, and mistakes and shipping delays are possible. You will have to deal with irate customers, so make as many backup supplies as you can to provide alternative products to your customers.

Platforms for Online Retail

Online retail platforms are a great benefit for dropshipping businesses, but they can also be a disadvantage because customers can bypass you and buy the same products directly from the retail platforms.

Shipping Can Be Difficult

Dropshipping companies typically source their products from a variety of suppliers and wholesalers. Shipping to customers can become complicated when multiple item orders are placed from multiple suppliers. You will then have a separate shipping charge for each item in the multiple product order, and you will not be able to pass on the additional costs to your customer; you will have to bear the additional costs. This reduces your profit margin.

Suppliers are not immune to errors.

Suppliers make mistakes, and when this occurs, you will be held accountable. The responsibility is yours because the customer placed the order with you rather than your supplier. Supplier errors can occur for a variety of reasons, some of which are legitimate, while others are the result of problems within the supplier's own company.

To avoid mistakes such as shoddy workmanship, subpar packing materials, and damaged or lost shipments, you must carefully select your suppliers. If your suppliers fail you due to negligence, you should immediately switch to a reputable supplier because these errors reflect poorly on you. Your company's reputation is extremely important, and you do not want to jeopardise it.

Suppliers' Scaling Capabilities

Not all suppliers are equally competent, and some may be unable to scale as your company expands. The good news is that you can source your products from suppliers all over the world as well as online retail platforms, making it very simple to switch suppliers.

CHAPTER 5

DIFFERENT DROPSHIPPING FORMS

DROP SHIPPING

The Dropshipping began as a very simple business model. It was more of a service than a full-fledged business model in which product manufacturers and wholesalers offered dropshipping to suppliers. When a customer placed an order for a specific product, the suppliers would ship it to them one at a time.

From there, the dropshipping business model evolved to the point where dropshipping is now a standalone complete business. We now have several variations of the dropshipping business model to meet the needs of individual businesses.

Suppliers' Information

This is the most personal version of the dropshipping business model, in which suppliers are contacted via phone and email. Terms and contracts, interactions with the support team, and all other negotiations are carried out with real people rather than automated systems.

Benefits

Business that lasts

Building long-term business relationships with suppliers results in a sustainable business. When problems arise or new products become available, your supplier is much more approachable and accommodating with this type of dropshipping. Many dropshipping companies prefer this type of dropshipping because they prefer personal relationships over the anonymity of e-commerce online retail platforms.

Mutual Benefits

It is normal for any business to have problems, and having a personal relationship with a supplier alters how those problems are resolved. Working together to solve problems in a positive way benefits both the supplier and the dropshipping company. It's not just that you lost a sale and made no profit. The supplier is well aware of the impact that each lost sale has on his own company.

Drawbacks Difficult to Find

When you use online retail platforms, everything is impersonal; you approach any of the numerous online platforms that are easily accessible via the internet. When using suppliers, you must put in a lot of effort to find a supplier you can fully trust, who is professional and dependable. If your supplier goes out of business, you're stuck until you can find another reliable supplier.

Errors Made by Humans

Human error can be disastrous for a dropshipping business. Suppliers who are not vigilant and keep tight control over their inventory may have far-reaching consequences for you and your company's reputation.

When an e-commerce order is placed, it creates a legally binding contract between you, the seller, and your customer. It is considered completely unprofessional for a seller to cancel an order, and the customer will leave a negative review on your website and on social media.

When this occurs, the dropshipping seller attempts to avoid it by placing an emergency order for the specific item on one of the online retail platforms or an alternative supplier, usually at a higher price. You must notify your customer of the delay in shipping their order, which may result in the loss of a returning customer.

Relationships Are a Lot of Work

When you use suppliers for your dropship business, you must maintain constant communication. You can't build a strong working relationship with your suppliers if you only communicate with them via phone, email, and whatever chat apps they use. This is time-consuming, and some people dislike it because they prefer the fast, automated communication provided by online retail platforms.

Establishing a Store on an Online Retail Platform

Using an online retail platform is the simplest and quickest way to get your dropshipping business up and running. It is critical to understand that not all online retail platforms operate in the same way. Each platform has its own set of rules and policies.

You must conduct research on each of these platforms to determine which one meets all of your specific needs, is the most cost effective for your dropshipping business, and provides the most benefits.

Timeline for Setup

The major retail platforms promise to have your store up and running within 24 hours, which is a huge plus. First-time entrepreneurs are still trying to find their footing in their business venture and frequently lack the knowledge and resources to get started on their own. As a result, being able to visit their store and begin organising and selling in such a short period of time is extremely valuable to them.

Audience in the Present

Instead of laboriously setting up their own website and struggling to gain decent search engine ranking, they can gain immediate access to a large audience in their niche. E-commerce can be intimidating to inexperienced dropshipping business owners because most start with an idea that they want to grow into a profitable business. Your chosen niche may be fantastic, but the complexities of the process can be overwhelming.

Having access to everything that retail platforms have to offer makes taking the first steps into dropshipping more manageable.

Marketing

Unless you are an experienced professional marketer, marketing can be a nightmare for most people. Outsourcing your company's marketing is expensive and consumes any funds you have set aside, money you could spend much better on other aspects of your business. Signing up with your preferred online retail platform relieves you of the enormous burden of marketing.

Possibilities for Apps and Automation

Dropshipping from online platforms allows you to access a large number of apps that you would not be able to access for free or at a low cost if you had to invest in these apps for your own dropshipping website. E-commerce is heavily reliant on apps, and in today's competitive markets, many apps are required to keep a business running smoothly.

Drawbacks

Many disadvantages of selling through retail platforms are unique to how they operate. However, there are some general drawbacks that affect your cash flow, are time consuming, and can have a negative impact on your business.

Several Fees

When you dropship through retail portals, you will incur a number of fees, which can quickly add up. Some platforms charge more depending on how the specific retail platform operates. You should be aware of the following fees:

- Subscription fees that vary depending on the plan you select and the benefits of specific plans.
- Fees for listing
- Fee for final value (eBay).

There is no true individuality.

The online retail portal controls the appearance of your store, as well as the marketing and branding. There is no room for uniqueness or customization.

There is no contact with customers.

You do not build rapport with customers because there are no personal interactions. To them, you're just a disembodied e-commerce store on a computer screen. You do not establish long-term relationships with customers, and they believe they owe you no loyalty or consideration.

Not Creating an Asset

Your business is an asset in which you have invested time, energy, and money. When you dropship through suppliers and your own website, the business becomes an asset with a monetary value if you decide to sell it later. When you close your account, your online store on the retail platforms ceases to exist.

Dropshipping Arbitrage

This type of dropshipping has recently received a lot of attention and is being hotly debated. Arbitrage selling is not permitted on online retail platforms. To choose this type of dropshipping, you must first understand how it differs from others and all of the advantages and disadvantages that come with arbitrage selling.

Arbitrage dropshipping is essentially pitting one retail platform against another. Arbitrage sellers do not find suppliers and then list their products on the retail platform in their stores.

Platform A, for example, lists a product for $10, while Platform B lists the same item for a higher price. The arbitrage seller purchases the product at the lower price on Platform A and provides the buyer's delivery address on Platform B. Platform A then delivers the product to the customer of Platform B. The arbitrage dropshipper keeps the difference between the listed lower and higher prices.

Benefits Several Suppliers

For the majority of e-commerce products, there will be multiple suppliers on the retail platform listing the same products, though prices may vary from supplier to supplier. This means you can easily switch between suppliers based on who has the specific product you want at any given time. You keep your customers happy because they don't have to wait for stock or a delivery delay.

There will be no delay in entering the market.

Everything you require is already present. You don't need much time to set up a website and build relationships with suppliers. You simply need to compare the prices for specific items across retail platforms before you can begin accepting orders.

Automation

With the wide range of automation tools available, most aspects of your business can run automatically once you've set up shop, leaving you with more than enough time to provide excellent customer service.

Disadvantages Sustainability

In the long run, this type of dropshipping is not a viable business model. The ease with which anyone can set up this dropshipping business model attracts a large number of people who want to make the most money in the shortest amount of time. Profit margins are shrinking as a result of the fierce competition. This means you must aim to sell more and more in order to break even. With such a low profit margin, there is no room for cancelled orders or delivery issues because you simply do not have the cash flow to handle these issues.

Without automation, this is not possible.

The competition in this type of dropshipping is so fierce that it is no longer feasible to do so without utilising every available form of automation. You are competing not only with other companies in your specific niche, but also with bulk sellers who list literally thousands of products, including your niche products. Basically, everyone is jumping on the bandwagon, and there is only a finite amount of profit to be made, so individual profits continue to shrink.

Not in Retail Platforms' Best Interests

Arbitrage dropshipping has become highly contentious for online retail platforms due to the negative impact it has on their customer base. The platforms are not opposed to the dropshipping business model, but rather to arbitrage dropshipping, which pits one platform against another.

Customers can see that there is a flood of people doing arbitrage selling. Customers begin to investigate when their purchase from Platform B is delivered in Platform A packaging. They then change which platform they use for future online purchases.

Making Use of Amazon Fulfillment Service

Dropshipping on Amazon is legal, but the traditional form of dropshipping is discouraged. Dropshipping businesses have always gotten their products from suppliers who specialise in their niche. The supplier is responsible for the physical handling of the products, as well as the storage, packaging, and shipping.

Using the FBA system, the dropshipping company must purchase minimum order sizes from the original supplier, which is then stored in one of Amazon's warehouses. Instead of the original supplier from whom you purchased the products, Amazon becomes your dropshipper.

By taking over the functions that the supplier would normally perform, the FBA system provides numerous benefits to the dropshipping company. You, as the reseller, have access to all of the features and tools available to all Amazon store owners, as well as being a part of the world's most recognisable brand.

Many entrepreneurs are intimidated by the dropshipping model. Instead of the traditional dropshipping model, which has very low startup costs, they must invest in inventory and face many costs that they may not be financially prepared for when they first start out.

Please see Chapter 10 for complete information, fees, and policies regarding the Fulfilled by Amazon dropshipping business model.

CHAPTER 6

FIND YOUR NICHE

For a dropshipping company cannot be successful if you offer general products across a broad spectrum. Simply put, there is far too much competition from retailers, other e-commerce companies, and online retail platforms.

What Exactly Is a Niche?

You must specialise and focus on a specific product or niche, and you must only focus on products that fall within your chosen niche. It is simply not economically viable for a dropshipping business to scavenge for products that catch the eye or a popular trend at the time.

Determining which niche to specialise in among the nearly countless niches available globally can be difficult, and deciding on one specific niche to specialise in can feel overwhelming for anyone new to the dropshipping business model. We will walk you through the best guidelines that will greatly assist you in finding the niche that is right for you.

What are you passionate about and what piques your interest?

Make a list of things that you are passionate about, things that pique your interest, and that could be a niche for your dropshipping business. It is critical to select a niche to which you can relate. You must understand the product and sell with confidence to customers, knowing that you will be able to advise them professionally if they have questions.

If you are passionate about the niche you choose, you will be more perseverant and determined to succeed even when difficulties arise. If you don't care about the products you sell, quitting at the first bump in the road will be far easier.

Many dropshipping businesses began as a hobby of the owner and grew into a successful business where products are offered to people with similar interests.

Your success is dependent on your ability to conduct research.

It's one thing to be passionate and knowledgeable about the niche you want to work in, but you're also starting a business that has to be profitable. In order to determine whether your niche will generate an income stream for you, you must conduct extensive research.

Examine the Best Products in Your Niche

Search for the products you want to sell in your dropshipping business on websites such as ClickBank, Simple Goods, and Selify, for example. The more niche products you find on offer, the better because it demonstrates a demand. If you discover that none of your niche goods are available on these websites, it indicates that your niche products are not in demand and have not been successfully monetized by someone else.

Google Apps

Search for keywords and keyword combinations related to your niche using Google Keyword Planner and Google

Trends. Google tools will show you how frequently your keywords are searched in search engines. Google tools provide a variety of search options for you to explore and determine the demand for your niche products through people's searches.

Google Trends examines trends in online searches and tracks changes in the volume of searches over time. Google Trends statistics show any seasonal trends for the product search terms you used. This gives you a good idea of whether your nice products will have periods of high demand and then slow down at other times of the year, indicating that income from your niche products will fluctuate.

Google Trends also provides information on where people search for keywords related to your niche products.

The Internet of Things

Social media is extremely powerful and can be extremely useful in determining which niche will work best for you. Examine what is being said about your niche on Facebook, how people are talking about it, and look for groups and forums.

Shipping Fees

Shipping costs have a significant impact on your profit margin. If it is too high, your markup will cause your selling prices to skyrocket, and prospective customers will seek out cheaper options elsewhere. Low shipping costs can also be used as a marketing strategy and promotional tool if you can absorb the shipping costs rather than passing them on with a significant price increase. Customers are immediately drawn to free shipping, which leads to an increase in sales.

Profitability

It is critical to remember that the amount of effort required to sell a low-cost item is the same as the effort required to market a high-priced item. It is therefore worthwhile to seek out a niche with high-end products, as this will increase your overall profit margin.

Dimensions and Weight

Too often, when deciding to start a dropshipping business, people overlook the physical size and weight of the products they want to sell. Shipping costs are inconvenient, and everyone attempts to avoid them at all costs.

This is critical because if your chosen niche products have high shipping costs, your profits can quickly vanish.

Legal Promotion

Investigate the products you want to sell thoroughly to ensure that you will not face any legal issues. You must be able to sell your niche products in any location. It is critical that you can sell on online retail platforms, your own website, and through social media without fear of being shut down for violating any state or country laws.

Impulse Purchasers

A large percentage of online shoppers see something they like and buy it on the spur of the moment. People's shopping habits have shifted as a result of having the entire world at their fingertips when they shop online. This should be considered when selecting your niche, and the products you sell should be appealing to impulse buyers.

Selling products that appeal to impulse buyers allows you to significantly expand your customer base right away. Yes, it is true that most impulse buyers do not become repeat customers. When you calculate how much income you generate through this type of sales over time, you will be surprised at how much it adds up to.

Strategy

Personal Interest

When you are genuinely interested in something, your general knowledge of the subject will be far more extensive than if you choose a niche and products in which you have no interest and no knowledge. Beginning your product search with a strong foundation of interest and knowledge will make your search more productive. You will be able to discard products that you are not passionate about, as well as low-quality products that will not sell well.

Professional Background

Another strategy for finding the best products to sell is to look at things from the perspective of someone who has professional experience with such products. You may not be enthusiastic about the products, but you do understand how they work and what their advantages and disadvantages are. You may have come into contact with the products as a result of your own interactions with them or as a result of your job. The important thing here is that you will be able to confidently answer customer questions and provide knowledgeable and factual answers. Another advantage of selecting products from a professional standpoint is that you will be aware of market gaps and areas where there is a clear need for products in that industry.

Trends vs. Fads

Fads come and go, and what is popular today may be obsolete tomorrow. Your goal is to make money, so in order to capitalise, you must first be able to distinguish between fad and trend. Fads are gimmicks that are unnecessary and quickly forgotten.

When considering trendy products for your niche, ask yourself two questions. Does this product meet a need for people? Does it solve a problem for users? A trend meets a need or solves a problem, whereas a fad is interesting or fun for a few weeks or months before people become bored and move on to something else that piques their interest.

What irritates and irritates people?

Put yourself in the shoes of a customer when researching your products. What are people's annoyances and frustrations that they have to deal with on a daily basis? The criteria is to find products that will make life easier for customers and that they will want to buy.

Others' Hobbies and Interests

You do not have to be personally interested in a subject; instead, conduct research into other people's hobbies and interests to see if there is a market for products related to their interests. Searching for hobbies, top hobbies, or trendy hobbies is a good place to start.

Going through hobby magazines, particularly those dedicated to specific hobbies, is another great source of information. Going through social media groups is another research tool. Look at what they're saying, what they're buying, and the jargon they're using. Make a list of words that are specific to a hobby; these are valuable search terms to have on hand.

Learn about people who have specific hobbies, because everything you learn about your potential customer base can be used to develop marketing strategies for products that they are particularly interested in.

Availability in your area

To make your dropshipping business financially viable, you must carefully select your niche. If your niche products are available freely at local retailers, people will simply pop out and pick up the items from their nearest shop. Humans are impatient, and they will not wait for products to be shipped to them if they can pick them up on their way home from work.

You have access to global markets, which greatly expands your supplier base, and with research, you will be able to find a great niche and products that customers want that are not available in local stores.

Examine What Your Competitors Are Doing

It is easy to fall into the trap of believing that if there is little or no competition for the niche you desire, this is fantastic and you will dominate the market in your niche. Conduct some research to see who your competition is, because there are usually good reasons why other companies aren't offering these specific products.

The reasons range from the fact that there is simply no demand for these products to the fact that there is so little profit to be made that other companies have moved away from them. It could also be that the shipping and packing costs are prohibitively expensive, or that production issues are so difficult to resolve that investing in these products is not profitable.

When deciding on the best niche for you, you must consider all of the above factors. You may not enjoy competing, but competition means that your products are in high demand, and with these products, your company will be sustainable in the long run.

CHAPTER 7

SEEK OUT AND SECURE
TOP-NOTCH SUPPLIERS

Not all suppliers are created equal; some are exceptional or good, while others are mediocre or worse. This is the reality that all new dropshipping companies face, and you must know what to look for right from the start suppliers, how to deal with suppliers, and what to avoid

Before contacting suppliers, ensure that you are legally permitted to do so.

When you begin sourcing and contacting potential suppliers and wholesalers, you must have all of your paperwork in order and your business properly set up in all legal aspects. This is critical because suppliers will require proof of your legality before doing business with you.

It is acceptable to begin by asking basic questions; suppliers are accustomed to entrepreneurs seeking information and will provide you with answers without demanding proof that you are a legal company.

Suppliers and wholesalers will not do business with unapproved companies, and in order for that approval to be granted, you must be legally incorporated and have followed all state laws. Unfortunately, wholesalers have discovered the hard way that far too many people attempt to defraud them. So, make sure all of your paperwork is in order, and you'll be on your way to developing positive relationships with your suppliers.

Suppliers Successfully Found Online

Suppliers and wholesalers are notorious for being eccentric and highly individualistic, and finding the ones with whom you truly want to do business will necessitate some creative searching. Suppliers do not try to avoid entrepreneurs; they simply march to the beat of their own drummer.

To achieve the best results, you must conduct thorough research and follow the guidelines outlined below.

Extensive Searches

Suppliers do not place a high priority on marketing their products. You'll have to sift through a large number of search results to find the information you're looking for. When searching for a specific product, the official website of the supplier is frequently found on Page 6 or Page 10 of the search results. Persevere, and you will be rewarded.

Change Your Search Criteria

You must modify your searches; simply searching for supplier X or product Y will not suffice. At best, your search results will be mediocre. Make a list of synonyms, such as wholesaler and supplier, and then conduct a search on each of the synonyms. To get the best search results, try different wording and search phrases.

Not aesthetically pleasing, but functional

When you visit a website, you usually look for things that appeal to you, items that catch your eye right away, and websites that keep your attention with catchy web content and high-quality photos.

Wholesalers and suppliers have minimalistic and functional websites that often appear quite old fashioned and antiquated, especially to young entrepreneurs. They are fully aware that clients require them and will seek them out, so they do not waste valuable time and resources creating websites to entice potential clients. Learn to look past their websites' outward appearance; it is not an indication of a bad supplier or mediocre products on offer.

The Benefits of Paid Supplier Directories

Using supplier directories is a hotly debated topic because some people believe it is an unnecessary extravagance that you won't use again once you've chosen your suppliers. There is no right or wrong answer; it is a personal decision made by each entrepreneur.

These databases are extremely useful to have on hand because they are organised and categorised so that you have all of the suppliers for specific products together and are regularly updated. Most of the top organisations that provide paid supplier directories also screen the companies before listing them to ensure that all of their listings are legitimately operating suppliers and wholesalers.

Another advantage of using paid directories is that you have access to a large number of alternative suppliers for your niche products in the event of an emergency that requires you to switch suppliers quickly.

Supplier directories are not a must-have for your business, but they are a reliable and convenient tool to have when you need it or want to start scaling your business.

A Pro Tip to Keep in Your Toolbox

When you're in a bind, you can use the well-known trick of placing a very small order with one of your dropshipping competitors. This can be extremely beneficial if you have been unable to locate a supplier.

Once you've received your order from your competitor, you can quickly and easily do an internet search of the return address on your package to find out who originally shipped it to you.

Increase your supplier's credibility.

Credibility is a valuable currency in the ever-changing world of e-commerce, and it is essential for the success of your dropshipping business. To appreciate the significance of this, imagine yourself in the shoes of suppliers and wholesalers. They are constantly dealing with eager entrepreneurs who may or may not become their clients. They do not have the time or inclination to deal with people who are unsure of what they want and frequently attempt to use the supplier as a free sounding board to answer questions and provide free advice.

When approaching a supplier, be decisive and professional. Do not be vague about your business objectives, and do not begin requesting terms and discounts before you have even begun placing orders with them.

Credibility cannot be demanded; it must be earned over time through interaction with the supplier. If you are overbearing and demanding when you are just starting out with a supplier, you will be labelled as an annoying upstart who should be avoided at all costs, and you will find it difficult to shake that negative reputation.

Pick up the phone and talk to someone.

We live in a world of instant communication via email, chat programmes, and social media, with no personal contact with others. Change your mindset when looking for a new supplier and make personal contact by picking up the phone. Speak with them, hear their voice, and you will discover that people are far more approachable than impersonal words on a screen.

Suppliers are used to answering customer questions and will accommodate you, which will help you build a good rapport with the supplier. Make a list of questions you need answers to if this is a new supplier and you are nervous about approaching him for the first time.

Place Orders for Tests

When you want to place orders with a new supplier, it makes good business sense not to jump in blindly, because even if you have done extensive research and are confident in the supplier's ability to complete order fulfilment successfully, you should test the waters.

Place small orders for the first few orders so you can

observe how this particular supplier or wholesaler runs his business. This will allow you to see how well the company handles the ordering process and how long it takes to ship orders to your customers. Take note of how quickly the supplier provides tracking information and how quickly the company's billing department issues an invoice to you.

You can solicit feedback from your customers about the packaging they received and assess their satisfaction with packaging, shipping, and delivery.

Supplier Qualities to Look for

When choosing your suppliers, make certain that they are reputable and dependable. You cannot put your company's success in the hands of a supplier who is careless or has a reputation for being late with shipments. Suppliers are essential in any dropshipping business, and you must be confident that the supplier is trustworthy. So, when determining whether a specific supplier will successfully perform his role, use the criteria listed below as a yardstick. What you should aim for is that your intended supplier has the majority, if not all, of the required characteristics.

Members of Staff Who Are Well-Trained and Informed

Competent suppliers with experienced staff who can answer questions about the products they sell professionally. If the sales staff is unable to fully answer questions about the industry they represent or the various products they market, it reflects poorly on the supplier's ability to run a well-managed business. You need a supplier on whom you can rely, especially if you are a new business or are expanding into a new niche in which you do not have extensive knowledge.

Modern Technology

E-commerce in all of its forms is heavily reliant on modern technology. Check to see if the prospective supplier has kept up with the technology required to ensure a smooth ordering, shipping, and delivery process.

The supplier's website does not need to be fancy; rather, it should be extremely functional, so see if he has invested in the following online trading necessities.

- Online catalogue that is all-inclusive.
- Data feeds that can be tailored to clients' specific requirements.

- Real-time inventory is available.

If you are using suppliers from within the country, consider the location.

When using locally sourced supplies, you should consider where the supplier is located. The more central the supplier's location is, the better it is for your company. Local shipping is well-known to take significantly longer than shipping into the country from abroad. If your supplier is central, you will save a lot of time on shipping. Less shipping time often equates to lower shipping costs and happier customers.

Ordering Method of Preference

Discover the various methods by which the supplier accepts orders. You do not want to be limited to placing all of your orders over the phone. This is inconvenient because you are limited to business hours only.

If you are only able to place orders manually through the supplier's website, the ordering process is slow and time-consuming. You require the third option of placing orders via email in order to free up time that you can use productively on other tasks.

You will be dealt with by a dedicated support staff.

It becomes very frustrating if you have to deal with a different support staff member each time you call the supplier. You have to repeat yourself because the staff you deal with has no idea why you called the first time. When you need to solve a problem, this is extremely inconvenient and time-consuming. A reputable supplier will assign a dedicated support representative to handle your orders and inquiries.

Avoiding Suppliers and Wholesalers

There are several telling signs that you should avoid a particular supplier or wholesaler. Look for another supplier who runs his business ethically and does not pressure clients with deceptive schemes. As soon as you notice any of these signs, be cautious and avoid getting involved with suppliers.

Negative Feedback

Examine the supplier's website for negative feedback from previous customers, and look on social media to see how many complaints clients have had. Consumer complaint websites provide a good indication of a supplier's reviews and feedback.

Products in Large Quantities

Companies that specialize in the sale of extremely low-cost bulk products do not inspire trust as a preferred supplier for your dropshipping business.

Demanding Ongoing Fees to Do Business With Them

Suppliers who charge you monthly fees for the "privilege" of doing business with them should be avoided at all costs. This is a form of coercion that you should avoid.

Exceptionally High Pre-Order Fees

Pre-order fees are a fact of life for all dropshipping businesses, and these fees vary depending on the size of the order, whether it is a bulk order or a very complex order. What is not normal is a supplier who charges far higher than average pre-order fees; this is not an ethical business practise.

Policy on Non-Negotiable Minimum Size

If a supplier is unwilling to be flexible with his minimum order size policy, this company is not a good fit for your dropshipping business. Many suppliers are willing to charge you the minimum size fee up front and then fulfil your order quantities as your customers place orders with you over time. Before you begin working with a supplier, make sure you understand what to expect.

CHAPTER 8

SHOPIFY

Dropshipping businesses rely on online e-commerce retail platforms as an essential component of their operations. The e-commerce online platforms do not operate in a standardised manner; each has its own operating methods as well as advantages and disadvantages. For a variety of reasons, Shopify is one of the most popular platforms to use.

What exactly is Shopify?

Shopify is an all-in-one online retail platform. You create an online store on the platform for a monthly subscription fee, from which you can market and sell your products globally. Shopify has put together an impressive set of tools to help you set up your store, including the integration of multiple payment gateways and support for more than 50 languages.

Shopify provides round-the-clock support to all customers, including 24/7 phone support and live chat to assist with any issues that may arise.

The Advantages of Using Shopify for Your Dropshipping Business For Newcomers

For anyone starting out in the dropshipping business, the e-commerce platforms can be overwhelming, but Shopify makes it as simple as possible. They provide tools to assist you in setting up your Shopify account and are extremely dropshipping friendly.

Shopify regularly posts tutorials to help customers learn how to use the retail platform, as well as case studies to help people with questions. They also post success stories on a regular basis to encourage new entrepreneurs who may be hesitant to start a business.

Templates and Themes, Both Free and Paid

Shopify offers a wide range of professional themes and templates that are ready to use when you create your Shopify store. The templates are customer-focused and mobile-friendly. All of the templates are extremely responsive and simple to use. The fact that you are not limited to only paid for templates and themes is a huge benefit for someone just starting out in dropshipping. The free templates work great, and you don't have to spend any money right away. If you want more extra features and enhanced customization, you can upgrade to paid themes and templates at a later stage.

SEO Functions Are Included

All forms of e-commerce are highly competitive and rapidly expanding. To succeed, you need all the assistance and support you can get. Most entrepreneurs are not SEO experts, and this can be a time-consuming aspect of their business. Shopify does all of the legwork for you in terms of SEO by providing you with all of the features you need to be visible to search engines and indexed. Today, search engine visibility is a critical requirement for any business.

The following features are available for use:

- Meta tag creation and modification.

- Product descriptions can now be added.

- Organizing products into collections.

Cross-Channel Selling

The ability to sell across multiple channels is a huge advantage for your company. You can link your Shopify store to a Facebook page and use the Shopify app for direct sales to greatly expand your potential client base. As a marketing tool, social networking is extremely effective, and you can conduct cross-channel sales on other platforms such as Twitter and Pinterest. Conduct some research to identify platforms that support cross-channel sales.

A Comprehensive App Store

Shopify has created a large number of apps to assist their clients. These apps expand the capabilities of your Shopify store. These plugins and extensions allow you to select the ones that best meet your specific Shopify store needs. With over 1,500 apps to choose from, both paid and free, you can perform tasks such as stock availability and reporting, customer service, and connecting with social media much more easily.

All of these tools and apps are aimed at increasing your sales and potential customer base, as well as improving your online visibility.

Community

Even with the best support, problems arise in business, and you are unsure how to handle them. The Shopify community forum is a great place to ask questions, raise concerns, and get advice from Shopify users all over the world.

Language Assistance

The Shopify platform supports all languages, which is a critical feature. You can use the language of your choice for your store, checkout, and all email correspondence with customers.

Oberlo Pushes Shopify to New Heights

When Shopify acquired the Oberlo app in 2017, it shook up the entire e-commerce world, and all Shopify sellers reaped significant benefits. You can connect to Aliexpress, the largest online retail platform in China and the Far East, using Oberlo.

The Oberlo app is only available to Shopify sellers; it does not work with other online retail platforms.

Oberlo's Primary Offerings to Users

Customization

You can make extensive changes to your product descriptions, as well as change or add images and product titles.

ePacket Filter

This filter allows you to select items with the shortest delivery times and import only those items.

Lists of Desire

You can create multiple wish lists for Aliexpress products, and you don't have to switch over to import the wish list products – you can do so directly from your wish lists.

Dashboard for Sales Tracking

You can keep track of your costs, earnings, and sales using the sales tracking dashboard.

Several User Accounts

This feature provides you with versatility by allowing people other than yourself to manage your online store.

Existing Products Can Be Networked

If you already sell products on Aliexpress, you can link them to Oberlo.

Pricing Automation

The ability to create pricing rules so that you can price products in bulk rather than individually.

Shipment tracking

You can keep track of your orders at all times with the integrated order tracking.

Change Suppliers

You can easily switch from one supplier to another to take advantage of the best available prices.

Plans and Pricing

All new clients receive a 30-day free trial of the Pro Plan, which includes all of the app's main features without the need to provide credit card information. Billing begins only after the trial period has ended.

Starter Strategy

This plan is free with the following conditions and features:

- A maximum of 500 products may be sold.
- A maximum of 50 orders may be placed per month.
- Orders from customers are automatically filled.
- Your products will be synced on a daily basis.
- Reports on sales
- Pricing is done automatically.
- You can use the Oberlo Supply marketplace.
- Oberlo is a free Chrome extension.

The Fundamental Plan

The following features and stipulations are included in the fixed monthly price:

- You have the option of creating 10,000 products.

- Each month, a maximum of 500 orders may be placed.

- All of the benefits of the starter plan.

- Fulfillment monitoring.

- Shipment tracking.

Plan Pro

- Up to 30,000 products may be sold.

- Orders are not limited.

- All of the basic plan's features.

- Various stores with a large number of customers.

Advantages of Using the Oberlo App

- Access to an extensive list of Oberlo dropshipping suppliers with a track record of success.

- Importing from Aliexpress is safe, quick, and simple.

- To manage products, a high-tech dashboard with a user-friendly interface is used.

- Products can be personalised.

- Order fulfilment is automated.
- Significant time and labour savings.
- Additional scalability.
- Video tutorials and the Oberlo blog are available to help and guide users.
- Integration with your Shopify store in a single step.
- Your inventory and prices are automatically updated.
- Price increases.
- You can use the Oberlo supply marketplace.
- Tracking of sales and shipments.
- The ePacket filter.
- Despite the fact that only Aliexpress is supported, you can integrate Oberlo with your Amazon store.
- This is a free Google Chrome extension that simplifies the process of importing products and managing orders.
- The ability to quickly and easily switch product suppliers.

The Drawbacks of Using Oberlo

- Oberlo was created exclusively for use with Shopify. It is incompatible with other standalone websites or online retail platforms.
- Only Aliexpress is currently supported.
- Product editing is not possible within Oberlo; instead, you are redirected to your Shopify product description page.

Cons of Using Shopify

Shotify has numerous advantages, but, like any other online retail platform, it has drawbacks that all dropshipping businesses should be aware of before deciding on this platform.

CMS Restrictions

As a dropshipping company, your main focus is e-commerce sales, and you want to use a platform that gives you a lot of flexibility while also being simple to use. The Shopify CMS is not on par with, say, Wordpress, which is a major management system.

Shopify's content management system is designed for

running an e-commerce store, so you'll need to use a custom theme with customization options, as well as the Shopify blogging platform, for your dropshipping needs. SMS limitations can be overcome with modifications.

Content restraints

There are only two types of content to choose from: a page or a blog post. This is a problem when you want to link posts to specific products and it is difficult to generate any additional text fields for any of the products that you sell.

Product Lookups

The search capabilities of the entry-level Shopify plans are extremely limited, with no provision for advanced search filtering. You will need to upgrade your Shopify plan to gain access to the more advanced search features.

Payments

Shopify strongly discourages the use of payment gateways other than Shopify Payment. If you use any of the other payment gateways, Shopify charges a 2% transaction fee for each transaction processed through an alternative payment gateway.

Expenses

There is no online retail portal that provides their services for free. When you join Shopify, you must examine the various fees they charge in order to make an informed decision about which payment plan you can afford and will best suit your business needs.

Shopify provides you with a 14-day free trial period to familiarize yourself with the platform and get a better idea of what your specific business needs are.

To continue using the online retail portal after your 14-day trial period, you must select a subscription plan. The fact that they offer discounts for annual and two-year subscription plans is a plus. Each payment plan has its own set of benefits, with more features added to the higher-priced options.

There are currently five options available:

- Shopify Lite.
- The fundamentals of Shopify.
- Shopify.
- Shopify Advanced.
- Plus, Shopify (this plan has negotiable fees).

Scalability

Most dropshipping businesses begin small with the intention of scaling as resources and finances grow. When you reach the point where you want to expand, it is not easy to export everything you've done on Shopify because all content you've uploaded, as well as any features you've customised, is hosted by Shopify.

Your existing search engine ranking cannot be transferred to your new site. Your new site will have to start from scratch, be indexed, and rebuild its search ranking.

It is not impossible to export data to your new site, but it will require a significant amount of effort and time on your part.

The solution to the Shopify scalability issue is to build your own website when you first start your dropshipping business rather than relying solely on a retail platform. It takes more effort at first, but the long-term benefits are well worth it. Use the platform and gradually build your website alongside it so that when you need to scale, you already have your own website on a solid foundation with a CMS that provides all of the features of a major content management system.

Entrepreneurs Underage

To open your own Shopify account, you must be at least 18 years old. This is not a major disadvantage; rather, it is something that very young entrepreneurs should be aware of. If you are under the age of 18, your parents or guardians must open a Shopify account on your behalf before you can begin.

CHAPTER 9

EBAY

EBay is currently the largest online auction retail platform in the e-commerce marketplace. They cater to the needs of first-time sellers, infrequent sellers, major and bulk sellers, and dropshipping businesses.

Dropshipping Policies on eBay

- Dropshipping is permitted on eBay as long as the dropshipping company sources its own manufacturers, wholesalers, and suppliers.

- eBay does not permit you to list products on eBay that originate from any other platform, marketplace, or retailer that ships products directly to your customers, implying that eBay does not permit arbitrage dropshipping.

- The dropshipping seller must guarantee that delivery from his supplier will occur within 30 days of the listing's end date.
- eBay holds the dropshipping company accountable for his customers' satisfaction with the items purchased as well as the safe delivery of purchases within the timeframe specified.
- If the dropshipping business does not follow eBay policies, the following punitive measures will be implemented against the dropshipping business:
- Listings have been cancelled.
- Listings are being terminated administratively.
- Listings may be demoted or removed from search results.
- The seller's ratings may be reduced.
- Buying and selling restrictions may be imposed.
- Protection for the seller or buyer will be removed.
- Suspension of the dropshipping company's account.
- In the case of accounts and listings that eBay has taken action against, all fees, both paid and

payable, will be forfeited.

- No fees will be refunded or credited to you once action has been taken against your account.

Work Efficiently and Successfully on eBay Dropshipping

Dropshipping profit margins are low, so you must be competitive to be successful on eBay. Your goal is to sell as many items as possible, but more selling means more work for you to list, process orders through your supplier, and ensure that each sale is delivered individually.

Streamline

Finding products within your chosen niche that you can list on eBay as bulk listings or listings with variations is the best way to streamline your eBay workload. This significantly reduces your workload because you only have to list these products once. If you're not sure how to use these listings, their help section has all the information you need. By adjusting the listing period, you can easily reduce the time spent re-listing your products.

Availability

Out-of-stock and discontinued items are a dropshipping company's worst nightmare. Your company cannot afford a string of negative reviews from dissatisfied customers, and a high volume of complaints is not ignored by eBay, which could jeopardise your eBay store. eBay has very strict rules regarding customer complaints and will terminate your account if you receive too many.

It is not difficult to avoid any of this. You must stay on top of things and receive daily stock updates from your suppliers. Check the stock movements of the products you order from your suppliers on a regular basis and take note when stocks run low.

Your reputation as a trustworthy seller is everything, and there is simply too much competition in e-commerce for you to overlook this critical aspect of your business.

Demographics of Customers

Your success on eBay is determined by a variety of factors. It's like putting together a puzzle. Each puzzle piece has a specific place and must fit perfectly. The demographics of your customers are crucial in this regard.

Create a profile of the people who would be interested in purchasing the specific products that you have to offer. Their age group is also important because it will most likely influence their daily routines. These demographics will give you an idea of what time of day and even which days they are most likely to shop on eBay. This will allow you to change the times and days when you list your products.

The Importance of Timing

The time of day, day of the week, and month are all important factors to consider when listing your products to attract the most customers. The goal is to attract as many customers as possible, sell as quickly as possible, and maximise your profits.

Peak hours obviously attract the greatest number of potential customers, and for many dropshipping businesses, this is the best way to go. For several reasons, this is both a benefit and a disadvantage.

- Because everyone wants to list during peak hours, you will face far more competition than during off-peak traffic hours.
- Because of the high volume of people on eBay during these hours, you may notice that the site runs much slower than usual, which can be a

major issue near the end of an auction. People browse eBay stores in search of the best prices and products, and if the site is slow, you may lose sales because customers may not get to your listings in time before the auction ends.

If you have done your demographic research into when your customers are most likely to browse eBay, your customer demographics will greatly assist you in avoiding overwhelming numbers of competitors and the peak hour rush.

To achieve greater success, you must strike a balance between potential income during peak hours and the time schedules of your target audience. It all depends on what you want.

your niche products are, and whether your target group is the average shopper who will be shopping when almost everyone else is, or whether they will prefer to make their online purchases at other times.

Customer Service

The customer is at the heart of any business, and your goal for your dropshipping business should be to not only attract customers, but also to have them return and place additional orders. It cannot be overstated how important it is to cultivate positive relationships with your customers.

The key to developing positive relationships is to establish a reputation for dependability. Customers must be able to trust that they will be able to obtain the products you have listed and that you will ensure that the parcels arrive quickly and in excellent condition.

If a problem arises, your customers must know that you will go to great lengths to ensure that you find solutions and that they are satisfied with the results. You cannot afford to be abrupt with customers, no matter how stressful a problem situation is for you, even if they are completely unreasonable and shouting empty threats at you.

Price Regulation

People want to pay the lowest possible price for whatever they are purchasing and will shop around for the best deals. Dropshipping companies may face logistical difficulties as a result of having to deal with all of the various fees, subscription costs, and prices charged by your suppliers. To make a profit, keep customers happy, and run your business efficiently, you must understand how these four basic variables affect your prices:

- Supplier prices are set.
- The final sales price varies.

- eBay charges two types of fees: listing fees and percentages of the final sale price.

- To effectively control prices while still making the highest profit possible, you should implement the following strategies and make the best use of options.

- Make use of the Buy it Now listing option. You offer your listed items at a fixed price, which allows you to make the profit you desired.

- Buy it Now has a set insertion fee that applies to both multiple and individual listings. The fixed insertion fee is typically less expensive than other listing fees.

- Setting a reserve price on a listing is another way to keep pricing under control. The reserve price is the lowest bid you will accept from customers on that specific auction item.

- When using the reserve price option, remember to adjust your reserve price to account for the fact that final value fees and insertion fees vary. The disadvantage of using reserved pricing is that your customers cannot see what the reserve price is, which can be very inconvenient for them.

- eBay provides a free calculator to help you calculate your various eBay fees. This is a very useful tool for saving time and reducing stress when calculating all of the fees and costs associated with eBay trading.

- To gain more control over your profit margin, you can choose to set a higher starting bid in order to cover fixed costs over which you have no control. These include your eBay listing and final value fees, as well as any supplier costs, taxes, and shipping costs.

Product Delivery

Keeping track of the entire fulfilment process is critical when competing with countless sellers on eBay every day. If your customers are dissatisfied, they will quickly find what they are looking for from another seller, and your reputation will be shattered.

Because you do not physically handle the products and rely entirely on your suppliers to complete fulfilment smoothly and quickly, the fulfilment process can be frustrating for any dropshipping business.

You want to find and keep suppliers who have their

finger on the pulse of their business and will keep you informed throughout the fulfilment process and will contact you immediately if there is a problem or the possibility of delays. This allows you to communicate with your customer before a situation escalates.

The Advantages of eBay Dropshipping Ease of Operation

Anyone with basic computer skills can easily negotiate on eBay. It is all set up.

to assist you in creating your store in the shortest amount of time and in making your store simple to operate You can use a variety of plugins and tools to help you.

Visibility

eBay is a massively popular online auction platform with a never-ending stream of visitors looking to buy anything and everything. This provides your eBay dropshipping business with the high visibility it requires to attract as many potential customers in your niche as possible.

Work Smarter, Not Harder

Because of the large number of daily eBay visitors who can view your listings, you have the potential to make sales with minimal effort and at the best possible prices.

Technical abilities are not required.

You don't need any technical knowledge to set up and run your eBay store. Everything is in place for you; all you have to do is focus on sourcing and listing your products.

Marketing

Because your company has access to such a large audience, you won't have to spend money on intensive marketing or invest in paid traffic and SEO. This is especially important when you are just starting out in the dropshipping business model.

System for Evaluating Fraud

The eBay evaluation system benefits both the seller and the buyer. Following the completion of each sale, both the customer and the seller have the opportunity to evaluate the experience, give a positive, neutral, or negative rating, and leave a comment about the specific sale, which aids in the prevention of fraud.

When customers leave out of the ordinary negative

evaluations, the evaluation system alerts you as the seller. You then have the option of rejecting the sale and explaining why it was rejected. Please keep in mind that this only applies in exceptional circumstances. Under normal circumstances, the seller is not permitted to leave negative remarks; the seller's only options are to provide praise and a review.

PayPal

eBay has integrated Paypal, allowing you to accept real-time payments and providing the seller with much-needed protection.

Ratings

Your eBay rating tells potential customers about your eBay credit rating, and eBay evaluates all sellers using three rating levels. The ratings are determined by the quality of service you provide as well as your sales history. The evaluation ratings are done once a month, and in e-commerce, the rating system can bring more customers, or it can have a very negative impact on your business if your rating is very low.

Best Rated

This rating informs all prospective customers that you have met the minimum sales target required for this rating. This rating also qualifies you for Top Rated Plus listing benefits as long as you meet the listing requirements.

Above Average

You've met the bare minimum of eBay requirements for all sellers, and your customer service is adequate.

Below Average

You have failed to meet one or more of eBay's minimum customer service standards. A low rating may result in eBay taking punitive measures, such as moving your listings to the bottom of the eBay search results.

The Downsides of eBay

Dropshipping Fees

When you have an eBay store, you must pay a variety of fees. When you sell through an online platform, you incur fees that you would not have incurred if you only sold your products through your own website. Because of competition, the profit margins on online platforms are lower, making listing fees an additional expense. If you sell products with add-ons, the fees will increase with each additional add-on you select.

Customization

You have no options for personalising your store in order to make it memorable to customers. Everything is standardised, and there are no options for inspiring customer loyalty through targeted product or niche marketing, or innovative sales techniques.

Competition in a Specific Market

If your chosen niche products are popular, you will face fierce competition from other sellers on eBay selling the same niche products, which could result in a price war between competing sellers.

Payments from Customers

Non-payment by customers is a recurring issue on eBay, as errors at the checkout occur frequently.

Monitoring

If you want to be able to sell enough products to make it worthwhile to open a dropshipping store on eBay, you must regularly monitor your listings. There are several tools available to help you monitor your listings to make this task easier.

Unfair Evaluations

Customers aren't always nice, and grumpy customers frequently leave angry, negative reviews that are completely unfair. This is a problem for any business, but eBay does not remove reviews, regardless of how unfair or out of context they are in relation to the problems that may have occurred. They will only remove a review in unusual circumstances. This creates a permanent record on your account, and if too many negative reviews are left, your account may be cancelled.

CHAPTER 10

AMAZON

Amazon is the world's largest online retail platform. Everyone is aware of Amazon and what they do. When you set up your dropshipping store and become a part of the Amazon brand, you are immediately associated with the Amazon brand. This alone brings significant benefits to your dropshipping business, even before you consider all of the other advantages of Amazon dropshipping.

Using the Amazon retail platform for your dropshipping business works in several ways, which we will go over in detail and explain how each type of dropshipping works.

Amazon's Dropship Policy

You can use Amazon FBA for dropshipping, which

essentially turns Amazon into your dropshipper because the products are shipped from an Amazon warehouse. You may also use other third-party suppliers, but you must follow Amazon's dropshipping policy at all times. If you do not follow the policy rules, you will face repercussions.

- You must always be the seller of record for all products sold on Amazon.

- You must be identified as the product's seller on all packing slips and waybills, as well as on any other information provided about the product or included with it.

- You are held accountable for accepting and processing all products returned by your customers.

- All other Amazon policies and the selling agreement must be followed at all times.

- You are not permitted to purchase products from any other online retailer and then have them delivered directly to your customers.

- On invoices, shipping orders, or packing slips, you are not permitted to include any information other than your own. All information indicating the seller's name and contact information must be yours, not that of another company.

- If you do not fully comply with this dropshipping policy, your account may be suspended and all selling privileges revoked.

Dropshipping Resources

There are numerous dropshipping tools that work with the Amazon platform. This can be extremely perplexing for entrepreneurs who are just starting their own dropshipping business. As you gain experience, you can investigate the various tools available. The tools listed below are essential from the start to allow you to do so much more to grow your dropshipping business and make it worthwhile to invest in.

Express Your Thoughts

You need as much positive feedback from customers as possible to increase sales and grow your dropshipping business. Feedback Express assists you in increasing positive feedback and removing negative feedback. This is the most effective way to keep your store and its products in high regard. Another feature of Feedback Express is the ability to blacklist customers who behave unethically by leaving unjustified negative reviews.

All Amazon sellers want to win the Buy Box because it

increases sales significantly. The metrics used to determine who wins the Buy Box are your feedback score and your seller rating.

This tool also sends alerts to your phone whenever a negative review about your service or products is left on your store's website.

This tool also includes personalised email templates with an auto insert function for images, logos, links, and order information to make things even easier for you.

FeedBack Express offers a 30-day free trial with the option to purchase at the end of the trial period.

FeedCheck

FeedCheck aggregates all of your product reviews so you can see them all in one place. This is a good tool to use if you have multiple listings because it allows you to see how each of your listings is performing and alerts you when you need to improve your customer service to boost your ratings. You can also use this tool to keep track of your competitors' products.

**There are three package options available.**

- Startup. This is intended for the new business owner who is just getting started as an Amazon reseller. This option provides a seven-day free trial period.

- Brand expansion. This is the best option for a company with a limited number of products to sell that are available from a variety of other sellers. You have a seven-day free trial period with the option to purchase.

- Enterprise. This is a better option for consumer goods corporations, agencies, and large brands. This package includes custom pricing options based on the number of products, an unlimited number of store channels, and client-specific requirements.

Merchant Phrases

The Merchant Words app gathers information from the Amazon autocomplete search bar about the words and phrases that Amazon users use when searching for products. The information is used to identify high-ranking keywords as well as product trends.

There are three subscription levels to choose from: silver, gold, and platinum. The following functions are available in the app:

Amazon data at the regional, national, and global levels.

- Monthly searches

- Keywords' seasonality.

- Collections of keywords

- Volumes of keyword searches

- Pge One examination.

- ASIN plus.

- History of keywords

- There are several users.

- Dashboard for a digital shelf.

- Keyword multiplier

- Metrics of performance

Amazon Volume Listing Instruments

Amazon has created a number of tools to help you manage inventory and order information more easily, including downloadable spreadsheets.

There are listing tools available to quickly change and modify product quantities and pricing.

Sellery

This is an Amazon repricing tool that works in real-time to adapt to marketing conditions by utilising a large number of price combinations to create a personalised pricing strategy for your Amazon store. Constant monitoring is accomplished through smart filters that react quickly to changes in order to keep you competitive.

Pricing begins at 1% of your monthly sales, with a minimum charge of $50 and a maximum charge of $150 per month. The product is available for a 14-day trial period.

Among the features are:

- Repricing has been scheduled.
- Repricing in real time.
- Pricing rules that are automated.
- Private labelling solutions.
- Pricing strategies that can be tailored to the needs of the client.
- Management of net margins.
- Expert assistance from Amazon.

- All of the features increase your chances of winning the coveted Buy Box.

Shopify

In 2017, Shopify announced an integration with Amazon. As a result, your Amazon store can now be added to Shopify as a sales channel on your website.

Store on Shopify. It only takes a few minutes to sync your Shopify products with your Amazon products. If you have Amazon sales that need to be fulfilled, Shopify will notify you. This integration creates a plethora of new sales opportunities for your dropshipping business.

Include a Product Tool

Rather than using bulk listing, this interactive tool is used to add each product one at a time to a small number of products. This web-based interface is best suited for the following tasks:

To create a new listing on Amazon for a product that does not yet exist. When you list a new, not-yet-for-sale product on Amazon, they create a product detail page for it.

To correspond to an existing product listing

The product you want to sell must be compatible with the existing product detail page.

Product Approvals and Limitations

Before you open your Amazon store, you must decide which category the products you want to sell belong to. It is critical that you read the restricted products help pages on the official Amazon website. Amazon's policies governing all products offered for sale on their online retail platform are extremely stringent.

Before you start your Amazon store or add new products to your store, you must be certain of which category the products fall into and what policies and laws you must follow. The consequences of not adhering to these policies are severe, and you may have your account cancelled and be barred from using Amazon in the future.

Amazon's products are divided into three categories.

- Products that are eligible but do not require approval.
- Restricted products that require approval, with some products requiring state or country-specific approval in addition to Amazon's own policies.
- Prohibited products will not be permitted to be listed on Amazon at all.

It is your responsibility as the seller to ensure that all of your listings are in good working order and that the time spent doing so is well spent. You worked hard to start your dropshipping business and deserve to reap the rewards, and there is no reason for your business to fail due to rules and regulations.

Fees for Sellers

Fees are a disadvantage that all sellers face, regardless of which online retail platform they use. Knowing exactly what seller fees you have to deal with and how the fees differ between selling plans allows you to decide which selling plan is best suited to your business and will have the least impact on your profit.

Please keep in mind that all of the selling fees discussed here apply only to sales in the United States. If you operate your dropshipping business from another country, you must confirm the fees that are applicable to that country.

You can choose between the professional seller plan and the individual seller plan, and the fees for each differ.

Fees Per Item

This fee applies to each item you sell on Amazon. Take note that if you use the professional seller plan, you will not be charged a per-item fee.

When you make a sale, Amazon collects the full amount paid by the customer. This includes shipping charges, per-item fees, any add-ons such as gift wrap, and any other extras requested by the customer.

Fees for Referrals

Every item sold generates a referral fee. A minimum referral fee per item is set for several product categories. When you sell a product that falls into the minimum referral fee category, you are liable for either the referral fee or the per-item fee, whichever is greater.

Shipping Costs

Professional sellers are responsible for shipping fees on media products when orders are not fulfilled by Amazon. Individual sellers are responsible for all shipping costs on all products sold. The shipping fees are calculated based on the item's category and the charges set for that category, as well as the charge for the shipping service selected by the customer. These shipping costs are borne by you, the seller.

When you use the Amazon FBA system, you will be charged FBA fees for services such as storage, fulfilment, and optional extras. This shipping fee is in addition to the fees associated with selling on Amazon.

Closing Fees That Vary

This fee applies to all media items sold by both professional and individual sellers. The fee is determined by predetermined fees for each category.

Professional Seller Strategy

- There is a monthly subscription fee.
- On each item sold, there is a referral fee that varies by category.
- Closing fees that vary depending on the category.
- This seller plan does not include the Amazon marketplace per item fee.
- Shipping charges are only applied to media products (DVD, video, video games, software, music, and books).
- Plan on selling more than 40 items per month.

Individual Seller Strategy

- This plan has no monthly subscription fee.

- Each item sold is subject to a per-item fee.

- Fees for referrals.

- Variable closing costs.

- Shipping charges apply to all items sold.

- This strategy is intended for monthly sales of less than 40 items.

Fulfillment by Amazon

Amazon introduced the FBA (Fulfilled by Amazon) dropshipping model in 2006. The FBA model functions in multiple ways.

As the seller, you ship your bulk purchases (minimum size orders from suppliers) to an Amazon warehouse, where they are stored and shipped to your individual customers as they place orders, and Amazon handles the packaging and shipping.

Dropshipping businesses also use the FBA service for products sold in their Amazon store, with Amazon handling fulfilment.

You can also use the FBA service to fulfil orders from other online retail platforms as well as products sold on your own website. Under the Amazon fulfilment umbrella, you combine your fulfilment from all of the different stores you operate.

The Amazon FBA shifts the goalposts for the dropshipping business model because it is no longer possible to dropship directly from your supplier to your customer. You must purchase inventory, even if it is only the minimum order size determined by your supplier, and that inventory must be stored in an Amazon warehouse.

Advantages of Using FBA Processing that is dependable and quick

Amazon is the world's largest retail platform, and it has a proven track record of being the best in the world at delivering a product to its destination as quickly as possible and in perfect condition, with no mishaps.

Increased Margin

Most suppliers will offer you wholesale prices when you buy products to store on Amazon, which is a savings over the prices suppliers offer you when you place individual orders with them.

Advantages of Amazon Fulfillment by Amazon

Amazon provides incentives to encourage you to list your products for dropshipping directly on Amazon.

Your conversion rate may increase if you are eligible for the following features:

- Super Saver Shipping is available.

- Prime membership on Amazon.

- Purchase the Box.

- Amazon handles product returns on your behalf by communicating with customers directly and shipping a replacement item to the client on your behalf.

Disadvantage.

Storage Fees

You must pay for your inventory to be stored at an Amazon warehouse. Dropshipping companies typically only store their best-selling products for FBA use because it is not cost-effective to store products with lower demand. Your suppliers do not charge you for storage because the products remain their property until you place an order.

Fees for FBA

Fees are charged for using the FBA service, which reduces your profit margin.

Fees for Long-Term Storage

On products that have been in storage for more than a year, you are responsible for the long-term storage fees. This fee is in addition to the standard storage fees that must be paid.

The long-term storage fee is calculated per cubic foot and per unit, and the applicable long-term storage fee is the higher of these two measurement costs.

There is no dedicated storage.

There is no dedicated storage space in the warehouse for your inventory. At Amazon, products from all suppliers are sorted into categories, so your inventory will be stored alongside products from multiple suppliers.

When it comes to shipping the product to your client, it may or may not be the item you purchased from your supplier.

To avoid having your items mixed up with the same product from another source, you could have an SKU-level sticker attached to your specific items, which costs $0.02 per item labelled. This may appear to be an unnecessary extravagance, but it ensures that your customer receives the exact item you purchased from your supplier, rather than an item that bears the same item name but may not be of the same quality as your originally purchased item.

The Advantages of Amazon Dropshipping

- You gain immediate access to the buying audience of the world's largest online retail platform, both locally and globally.

- The Fulfillment by Amazon system, which includes all of the advantages described in the section titled Amazon Fulfillment Service.

- Amazon ads reduce advertising costs because you can control how much you spend because Amazon does not have a minimum amount you must spend to use their ads.

- Reduced overhead costs for running your business.

- Automation for order processing, delivery, and marketing.

- There are tools for repricing products available, which eliminates the need to update manually.

- Buy Box if you want to achieve excellent ratings.

Disadvantages of Amazon Dropshipping

- Fees for listing

- Fees for warehouse storage if you use Amazon FBA.

- Extra warehouse storing fees for long-term storage if items are kept for more than 365 days.

- Vulnerability of your sales data because Amazon has access to all data pertaining to the operation of your store. This includes your overall sales totals as well as which of your items are your best sellers.

- Customization is limited because Amazon controls all aspects of your marketing and branding.

- The dropshipping policy establishes very strict guidelines for what a dropshipping business may and may not do.
- Punitive measures will be implemented if you fail to follow any of their policies.

CHAPTER 11

YOUR PERSONAL DROPSHIPPING WEBSITE

With all of the online retail platforms available to choose from, as well as the apps and plugins that everyone has access to, the dropshipping business model is incredibly flexible. This makes it quick and simple to get started with your dropshipping business. With all of the advantages of selling on retail platforms, such as templates, specialised apps, and marketing, many new entrepreneurs are content to use only these platforms. It's simple and straightforward, and you make money. This is fantastic, and all dropshipping businesses should take advantage of the available online retail platforms.

Why Is It Necessary to Build a Website?

This is the first question most people ask because it appears to be a lot of work for very little return. There are several reasons why it is critical that you begin building your own business website while using online retail platforms.

Your own website establishes your company's legitimacy in the eyes of potential customers, suppliers, and wholesalers with whom you wish to collaborate. It shifts the perception of you as merely a listing on a platform or a disembodied store among thousands of other online stores available on retail platforms.

Manufacturers and suppliers prefer to work with dropshipping companies that have a well-established website. Even if you're just starting out and have a small customer base, it shows your suppliers that you're serious about running a business and not just another fly-by-night dropshipping company looking to make a few quick bucks before closing up shop and moving on. When you approach new suppliers, they will look online to see if you have a website; your website helps you build trust and rapport with suppliers.

Your competitors are another important reason to create your own website. Dropshipping businesses that want to be visible and profitable have their own e-commerce websites. One of the most important aspects of e-commerce analytics is competitor analysis, and not having your own website can have a negative impact on the success of your business.

Setting Things in Motion

Not everyone is technologically savvy, and creating your own website is not something that everyone relishes. You need an e-commerce dropshipping website design that incorporates as many features as possible to make running your website simple and allow clients to navigate through your website without stumbling blocks caused by poor website design.

You have the option of having your website designed by professionals based on your specific requirements. You can use an internet search to find the appropriate templates and designs. There are numerous good website creation templates to choose from that will suit your niche and include features that address all of the specifics you require and desire for your own website.

Your budget will be the deciding factor in how you set

up your website, but the majority of the templates available will have free options. These free templates are more basic, but they will suffice if you are on a tight budget.

To begin, you must set up your website hosting, with WordPress website hosting being the most popular among users who use dropshipping extensions and plugins. Choose from a variety of design templates and a suitable domain name.

Hosting a website

It is critical to select the best and most beneficial web hosting service for your dropshipping business website. When you first start out, it can be difficult to remember what type of hosting is best and what to look for in a web hosting solution. People frequently throw up their hands and choose the first web hosting provider they find when conducting a search in order to avoid having to deal with this aspect. Some of the aspects to check may appear technical, but they are manageable with the right tools and time. To help you make the best decision possible, we've highlighted the most important features to look for when selecting your web hosting solution.

Reviews

Begin by conducting research on the web hosting services you are interested in. Unfortunately, websites that claim to publish factual reviews frequently let you down because web hosting services do not like negative reviews about their companies and will go to any length to remove these reviews from the sites where they appear. Do a Google search for the name of the company you want to learn more about and the word reviews, and you will get quick and accurate reviews from websites that publish unpaid reviews as well as information published on personal blogs of people who have used the specific hosting service.

Storage and Bandwidth Limits

Because you will be offering products from various suppliers, you will need a sufficient storage limit to run your dropshipping business. Your hosting service must be able to guarantee the easy and trouble-free upload of a minimum of 10,000 products.

Bandwidth is critical, so make sure you find out whether the hosting service has bandwidth limits or if it is unlimited. Customers will download information when they browse your store, and if your hosting service has limitations, this will cause problems, and customers will become impatient if they are unable to download information and images.

PHP 7 Compatibility and SSL Certificates

The presence or absence of SSL certificates on a site is one of the search engine ranking factors. Sites with SSL certificates rank higher. When customers browse, they may receive a Google popup warning that a specific website lacks SSL certification. This alerts the person browsing, and most will leave that site and go to one they believe they can trust.

Check that the web hosting service you select supports PHP 7, the most recent version of PHP available. This is especially important for your dropshipping website because some of the top dropshipping plugins no longer support all previous versions of PHP.

Pricing

Web hosting services can be very expensive, especially for a new e-commerce venture. Cloud hosting provides significant cost-saving benefits such as unlimited bandwidth and automatic scaling, which automatically adjusts when your website experiences an increase in traffic.

Performance

The performance of a hosting service can be measured using available tools to determine how fast or slow loading times are, as well as the actual page speed. Another option is to visit websites that use a particular hosting service and observe the loading times. This will assist you in removing hosting services that provide poor performance.

Security

The majority of hosting solutions now offer cPanel website management to their customers. Check to see if the hosting service employs cPanel or another lesser-known management system. You require a secure control panel that prevents all back-door entries and provides secure access via SSH and FTP.

Support for E-Commerce Platforms

Your hosting service should provide one-click installation of the top e-commerce online platforms.

Customer Support

A dependable hosting service will provide phone and email support 24 hours a day, seven days a week. Your company's success is dependent on prospective customers being able to visit your website at any time with minimal service interruptions.

Capability to Scale

If the hosting service you are considering does not offer automatic scaling, it is best to find one that does or ensure that their servers can be upscaled to meet your needs. Your company cannot afford to lose customers or reduce order placement due to the servers' inability to keep up.

Your Personal Domain Name

Your domain name serves as your address and is unique. Every computer on the internet has an identifying numeric IP address, but people will never remember a specific IP address among the billions on the internet. When it was realised that having an IP address was insufficient for finding specific websites, domain names were created. As a result, combining a unique IP address with a unique domain name results in a one-of-a-kind address. No company can afford to disappear in cyberspace; if they can't find you, they'll look for another company that does what you do.

Having your own domain name does more than just help search engines find your website; it has additional benefits that many people do not consider.

Internet Access Mobility

Once you've created your own domain name, it's yours. If you decide to leave your web host or switch servers, you can keep your domain name. You will face significant difficulties if you do not own your domain name. You'll have to start over with a different URL, and you'll lose all the work you've put into developing your brand name.

Credibility

If you don't have a domain name, your web host or ISP will assign you one. This is clearly visible on your web address and indicates that your company is not very professional or trustworthy. Humans are not the most trusting creatures, despite the fact that e-commerce has taken over the world. It is your responsibility to give them reasons to trust you and want to do business with you. Having a free generic URL indicates to others that you are unwilling to invest money in your online presence by registering a domain name.

No small business can afford to be labelled as cheap; potential customers will seek out other businesses that demonstrate a commitment to their mission.

It demonstrates that you are proactive.

Your domain name demonstrates that you are keeping up with technological changes. You don't want to alienate a large portion of your potential customer base by saving money by using generic URLs because the younger generations are very tech-savvy and pick up on the finer details.

Choose a Domain Name That Is Appropriate

You must not only select a domain name that is the same as your company name. If you choose a domain name that reflects what your business is all about, a word that connects online searchers to your niche, it attracts people who are looking for anything in your niche.

E-Commerce Website Requirements

You want your website to reflect your products and your niche, as well as to create a shopping experience for your customers that they will remember and make them return.

Product, design, and content must all be in sync.

You want your customers to associate your website with the products you offer, and they want this to happen. Every aspect of your website, from colours to text, images, videos, and music, must be tailored to your niche. Client demographics are also important; your website must appeal to the type of person who is interested in the products you offer.

Easy-to-Use Shopping Cart

Nothing irritates a shopper more than deciding to begin purchasing only to be stymied by a website shopping cart that makes it impossible to add, change, or remove products. When they want to return and browse some more, they get stuck and are unable to continue shopping. The customer is king, so take your time and consider all of the features that will make it a simple and stress-free process.

Keep the check-out process as simple as possible.

Your goal is to get your customers through the check-out process as quickly as possible because you need the highest possible sales conversion. Customers abandon the shopping cart for a variety of reasons before completing the transaction. Some shoppers do not complete the check-out process because they were only looking around and comparing prices. You have no say in the matter. Baymard.com researched and analysed what you can control, and the percentages of carts abandoned for each reason are eye-opening and clearly point out ways to make your website customer friendly and appealing.

Customers want their shopping experience to be simple and free of frustration. Your check-out process must be simple, smooth, and meet your customers' needs.

(Baymard Institute, undated)

The Internet of Things

Social media has become an essential part of millions of people's lives. Making social media a part of your website is critical in today's business world.

People nowadays check social media to see what is trending and what is being said about a product that they might be interested in. Using social media as a marketing tool draws a large number of people's attention to your products, resulting in a much higher conversion rate in sales.

Security

Your dropshipping website's e-commerce features must be of the highest calibre. The Payment Card Industry Data Security Standard (PCI DSS) is a data security standard that is required for any website that accepts credit cards.

Security is so important to shoppers that it is usually the first thing they look for on a website, and if the website is not secure, they will leave regardless of how badly they want to buy a specific product.

Making certain that your website design incorporates all necessary security measures serves as an incentive for buyers to become regular buyers of your products via your website.

Support for Multiple Languages

Many business owners do not consider the significant advantages of incorporating multi-language support into their website. This is more than just a customer convenience tool; it gives you a competitive advantage over competitors who do not offer multi-language support.

Multi-language support has been embraced by multinational corporations, but it is still largely ignored by smaller e-commerce. Because e-commerce has become such a large part of all international purchasing, smaller businesses can get a head start and reap the benefits while their competitors fall further behind.

This is a highly effective marketing tool that exposes your company to international markets and brings you new customers who are interested in your niche products. The ability to communicate in their native language will immediately capture their attention. When you include the top world languages, you increase your potential client base and have the potential to double your sales.

A multilingual website helps to break down cultural barriers and gain the trust of international buyers. People are often hesitant to make online purchases in a language they do not fully comprehend.

Most of the major search engines can conduct searches in languages other than English. With language support, you instantly increase the likelihood that your website will be found when people search for your products.

Plugins Are Required

You simply cannot run a dropshipping website without the use of plugins. You require them to handle the numerous tasks that would consume your time if you had to do them manually.

The plugins you require are determined by the online retail platform with which you have partnered, as some are platform-specific and will not work well on other platforms.

The goal here is to introduce you to the plugins that have received the most positive user feedback and have received the highest ratings. These are worth trying out to see which ones work best for your own website and products.

Dropshipping App Oberlo

This app is best suited for Shopify and is available in the Shopify app store. It has great features such as a list of approved dropship suppliers, which makes finding new suppliers a breeze. Since Amazon has a partnership with Shopify, this app is used to sync your Amazon sales channel with Shopify. The app offers a free option as well as two paid options.

Please see Chapter 8, sub-paragraph Oberlo Takes Shopify to the Next Level for a complete list of all the features offered by Oberlo.

Rabbit in Social Situations

This WooCommerce app is an automated tool for social media promotion of your website and business.

SEO Plugin

This plugin can be found in the Shopify app store. There is a free version as well as a paid version available. When there are any issues with how your website performs on search engines, the free version of Plugin SEO will notify you. It also covers fundamental SEO techniques.

AliDropship

AliDropship is a paid plugin that offers the AliExpress dropshipping plugin for WordPress. This plugin was created for users who import products from the Aliexpress marketplace. Because the majority of the features are automated, this plugin is extremely popular.

Woo Alidropship

This is the Alidropship plugin, which is a paid plugin designed to work with WooCommerce. This version of the plugin is more advanced because it has a newer design and more features, making it a better choice than the generic original version of the plugin.

Egg's Content

This tough WordPress plugin is extremely popular among users. Its purpose is to keep your product information up to date.

Product Evaluations

This WordPress plugin is used for product reviews and includes all of the standard features required for reviewing your available products.

Dropshix

There are two versions of this plugin. The basic option is free, while the advanced features option is not. Dropshix tracks shipments and generates real-time reports that are auto-synchronized. It comes with a Chrome extension built in.

MailChimp

MailChimp is an email marketing plugin that can help you with email marketing for your company. This is a useful tool for all e-commerce businesses that want to send out emails in bulk to notify customers about new products.

Options for Integration

It supports social media integration, such as Facebook, as well as access testing and scheduling to increase open rates. The fact that there are no restrictions on image hosting at no cost improves your marketing.

Templates

MailChimp provides several standard templates, but you can also import your own templates. You can also customise the standard templates provided with an easy point-and-click editor, eliminating the need for coding knowledge.

Logo

This plugin is available for free for up to 2,000 contacts. Their logo appears on both your subscription form and your campaign. The upgraded version of the plugin allows you to remove their logo from all outgoing mail from your company.

Metrics of Comparison

You can track your email campaigns and analyse how well they are performing. Another feature is the ability to compare your metrics to those of other Mailchimp subscribers.

No programme, plugin, or extension is perfect because it is impossible to design them to meet the needs of every single user. MailChimp addresses the majority of functions adequately, but there are a few drawbacks to be aware of before using this plugin.

Subscription and membership-based websites

The MailChimp plugin for WordPress sites, as well as PayPal, can be problematic at times. You will run into problems if your website offers membership and subscription options. You can also set up autoresponders, but the disadvantage is that autoresponders only work when people subscribe through one of your web forms and do not work with any contacts you have imported.

Templates are simple and standard.

The templates are simple and unappealing to the readers. To make the MailChimp templates more appealing, you must either spend time modifying them or import your own templates that are tailored to your customer demographics and products.

Problems with Interaction

It takes some time to become acquainted with the MailChimp interface, and some users find it difficult to use. This plugin is useful for businesses that send out information updates and newsletters, but it becomes time consuming if your email volume is high.

Another disadvantage of the interface is that you cannot send emails to multiple email lists at the same time. You are limited to sending out subscriber lists one at a time.

Account Suspension

If you receive spam complaints about your emails or a large number of unsubscribe requests, MailChimp reserves the right to cancel or suspend your account without informing you.

This means that users must be cautious and test emails before sending them to their subscribers in order to avoid suspension or cancellation.

The Benefits of Having Your Own Website Reputable Image

When customers visit your website, they will see that it has been designed to be professional and customer-oriented. People are more likely to spend money with a company that has a professional website rather than a listing on a completely anonymous retail platform.

There is no competition.

When you have to compete with so many other listings that sell the same or very similar products, it can be a pain. Visitors to your website will only see items that you sell. Prices on online auction platforms are frequently driven down to the point where there is no profit margin left because there are simply too many sellers competing. When selling on your own website, you can set realistic prices that allow you to make a reasonable profit.

Fees to List and Sell Disappear

If you offer PayPal and similar payment options on your website, you may still have to pay certain fees. You avoid many other fees that eat into your profit margin when you use online retail platforms, such as fees for each product you list, subscription fees, and more.

Disadvantages

Initial Start-Up Costs

When you start your own website, you will incur initial costs, so plan accordingly.

Make a budget for this. The initial financial outlay, however, is determined by the website you choose. Your start-up costs will be high if you want a custom-built website created by a web design company. When you choose to put in some effort, you can significantly reduce your costs with a WordPress website that provides you with a fully functional website that includes all of the necessities.

Support

You do not have access to the support staff that you do when you subscribe to online retail platforms.

You will be responsible for dealing with any issues that arise on your website. If, on the other hand, you chose a reputable website builder, you will have access to their technical support team to help you.

Slowly, traffic builds up.

It will take time to build organic traffic to your new website if you have just launched it. You will need to gradually build up your client base and loyal customers who will return to your website.

CHAPTER 12

IMPACT OF YOUR ONLINE PRESENCE

The significance of developing a strong online presence cannot be overstated. A company that does not have an online presence simply does not exist on the Internet. Even if your products are fantastic, search engines will not be able to find you. The more robust your online presence, the easier it is for search engines to find you when people conduct searches for your products and niche.

We will go over each of the strategies you should employ to achieve the best online presence possible, as well as how each strategy improves your visibility to search engines and prospective clients.

Marketing

Marketing can be likened to a finely woven spider web. It affects every aspect of your business and must all work together to improve your online presence, broaden your customer base, and increase your profit margin. Many aspects and forms of marketing are covered in detail in the paragraphs below, so this section will focus on other important aspects of marketing that were not covered.

Psychographics and Demographics

Google Analytics is a great place to start if you want to learn more about your customers' demographics and psychographics. These statistics are used to focus your marketing; otherwise, your marketing will be haphazard, hit-or-miss, and ineffective.

Demographic statistics provide information on your customers' age groups, family backgrounds, level of education, income, and location. Psychographics provide insight into your customers' motivations – why are they specifically interested in the products you offer?

All of these statistics enable you to create a customer

persona of what makes your potential customers tick. Google Analytics provides a wide range of statistics analysis, and you can add more to give you the most focused marketing efforts possible.

Customer Feedback and Ratings

The best way to build trust is to include a feedback page on your website and online store. Humans are not particularly trusting, and when shopping online, they frequently have reason to be. Use this scepticism as a marketing tool by including a section for customer testimonials and ratings, as well as a section where customers can leave reviews on your products and services.

Potential customers can read the reviews, as well as your comments on the reviews and how you resolved any issues. This type of customer interaction is the quickest way to establish trust and demonstrate to customers that you are willing to be completely transparent.

Trends in Marketing

Look into trendy and popular marketing strategies for reaching out to the broadest customer base possible in your niche.

Private messaging is available on all of the major social networks, allowing entrepreneurs to interact with their customers. You can communicate with potential customers directly on all of the social media platforms to which you have subscribed. Check your social media pages' private messages on a regular basis and respond to questions as soon as possible. This opens up a channel for marketing as well as customer service.

Another marketing trent to look into is live chat. Shopify provides assistance to users through a variety of live chat bot options available in their extension library. This option may not be ideal for a startup business that does not have the manpower to support live chat; however, it is something to consider for when your company has grown to accommodate this.

Chat bots are a marketing strategy that does not require human intervention. Customers can have their basic questions answered by bots without you having to be present.

Advertisements that are displayed

Display ads are a popular low-cost marketing option. Over the last decade, display advertising has grown and improved dramatically.

This type of advertising is now much more focused on your target audience and produces much better results than in the past.

There are two ways that display advertising works. You go to the top websites in your niche and see if you can buy ad space on them. This directs your advertising to people who are interested in your niche products. The second option is to work with a well-known ad network that will handle your display ads and placement.

Instead of reaching a large portion of people who are not interested in your niche products, the goal of display ads is to bring your brand to the attention of potential customers who fall into your niche.

Be where your niche congregates online.

Investigate where the people who would be your niche customers congregate on the internet. Wherever there is a niche, there will be blogs and social media groups. Join these groups and become an expert in your field. Examine what they say about your niche products and what their needs and desires are.

This is subtle marketing because you are not bombarding people with your company's information and advertisements. You are an expert in your field and can provide answers, pointers, and advice. Most bloggers and social media groups will gladly use your input and include posts you create while giving credit to your company.

Retarget

According to statistics, up to 98 percent of people do not buy the first time they visit a website because people like to window-shop before making any decisions. Instead of being disheartened by the low conversion rate for first-time visitors, consider it an opportunity for a different marketing strategy. According to statistics, retargeting customers with display ads can increase the potential conversion rate by up to 70%.

Retargeting marketing is currently underutilised for a variety of reasons. Some companies believe they do not have the time to retarget potential customers. Many entrepreneurs, particularly those new to the dropshipping business model, are simply unaware of this marketing strategy. This means that now is an excellent time to begin using retarget marketing because it will put you ahead of your competition.

Upsell and cross-sell

Cross-selling and upselling are two of the most effective marketing strategies for engaging impulse buyers because they are the easiest to persuade to make more than the one purchase they had planned on.

As a dropshipping company, your store and website are both silent. Your prospective customers are not confronted with eager salespeople offering helpful advice to upsell your products or cross sell by recommending other products that complement their selection. Cross-selling can be accomplished by grouping products that complement one another.

There are great plugins available for cross-selling and upselling whether you have an online store on a retail platform or sell directly through your own website. This marketing technique is supported by a number of plugins for Shopify, WooCommerce, and WordPress, as well as independent plugins.

Allow these plugins to be the voice of your company, with subtle pop ups based on the items visitors are browsing, as well as pop ups alerting them to additional products that they may be interested in.

Try out a few of the available upsell and cross-sell plug-ins to see which one best suits your marketing needs.

Marketing Strategies That Are Expensive

With so many low-cost and cost-effective marketing options available, using expensive marketing strategies is not an absolute necessity. If you have the financial means to invest in high-cost marketing, there are two popular options for your company.

Promotions and giveaways have always been popular with all types of businesses, and you can use these tactics to draw a lot of attention to your dropshipping business. It is worthwhile to consider this and see if you can fit it into your budget.

Influencer marketing has emerged as a result of social media. Because of the global popularity of social media, these influencers have a lot of power, and if any of them promote your products, it could significantly increase sales. If you are interested in this type of marketing, it is worthwhile to spend time researching which social media influencers would benefit your niche.

Branding

Branding is an important aspect of a dropshipping business that is frequently overlooked. Some people believe that having a dropshipping store on Shopify or listing on online retail platforms is sufficient to give them an adequate online presence.

Branding distinguishes your store from the crowd. Without branding, dropshipping on retail platforms makes you invisible. Yes, creating your own distinct brand takes effort and time; you have the option of being faceless in the crowd or standing out and being remembered. Your retail platform branding and your own website branding are inextricably linked.

Creating your own brand fosters trust; customers regard you as trustworthy because they can associate your company with your distinct brand. This is also an excellent marketing strategy.

Because you do not physically stock the products and your suppliers handle storage and delivery, branding for the dropshipping model differs from branding for other retail businesses.

Branding pervades your website, online store on retail

platforms, and social media. Your goal with branding is to ensure that people recognise your logo and associate it with your company in as many places on the internet as possible. Branding your dropshipping gives it a distinct and personal identity.

It is critical to understand that branding must evolve alongside your dropshipping business from the start. Trying to do branding when you have more time or feel more financially secure does not work very well. Attempting to retroactively brand yourself does not work well. You've lost too much ground because all of your previous customers have nothing specific to remember you by and will have moved on.

Advertising on Social Media

Social media began roughly four decades ago as newsgroups where people could communicate, and we are all aware of the enormous impact social media has on almost every aspect of people's lives. Taking your branding to social media gives you access to a massive audience that you can use for branding and advertising. With ad campaigns and your logo on everything, make your presence known on every available social media platform.

Using social media as a marketing tool for branding has another advantage. Every post you make on your Instagram or Facebook account generates organic traffic at a much lower cost than more traditional forms of marketing.

Here is a list of some of the advantages of using social media to boost your brand:

- Organic traffic at an extremely low cost.

- Because the majority of businesses ignore social media marketing, there is little competition.

- Pictures really do speak louder than words. Post videos and images related to your business and niche products to give people a better understanding of what you're selling.

- It is simple to set up and use social media accounts.

- There are no or very low advertising costs. Most social media platforms do offer paid advertising, but it is not required. You can effectively advertise on social media and reach a large audience. If you decide to boost your branding even further in the future, you can use paid ad campaigns.

White Labeling

Everyone is aware of how fiercely competitive the world's markets have become. Because white labelling is such an effective branding strategy, Amazon has pushed into it and begun offering their own white-branded products in order to increase profits.

It's a simple idea that works extremely well for a dropshipping business. You persuade your dropshipping supplier to white label the products you order from him with your own white label and logo rather than his own company labels. By changing the labelling, the supplier rebrands the product for you, making it "your" product. Many dropshipping suppliers are happy to do this because it allows them to continue selling their products under a different label. The most important thing for the suppliers is that no changes are made to their products, only the label.

White labelling is an additional marketing strategy.

When your suppliers rebrand your orders, you can negotiate with them to include a packing slip with your contact information, logo, and company policies as an extra marketing strategy.

Marketing for Packaging and Delivery

Another option that will help your branding is to include a brochure or mini-catalogue that will introduce customers to additional products that you offer.

Blogging

Blogging is big business these days, and it's an important part of your online presence that will help you with all aspects of your dropshipping business. To fully grasp the significance of having your own blog, consider that there are currently over 409 million people reading over 23.7 billion pages per month. The graph below depicts how reliable internet users obtain information from blogs.

FitSmallBusiness (2017, FitSmallBusiness)

It does not require you to be a world-renowned author or spend hours writing blog posts in order to be effective. Make it short and interesting, and compare it to posting on social media on a regular basis. Everyone spends time, and the majority of people do so on a daily basis, posting on various social media platforms about everyday issues.

Blogging is a business asset that can help you grow your business simply by doing what you already do on Facebook and Twitter.

The numerous advantages of blogging can be divided into four categories.

SEO Advantages

Every blog post you write creates a new page on your website. This is brand-new, one-of-a-kind content that has never been indexed by search engines. With each new blog post, your ratings rise and you become more visible when people search for your keywords, resulting in increased traffic to your website. The freshness of the content is one of the factors search engines look for, and blogging keeps the search engines fed.

When search engines crawl your website and discover only stale content, the time between crawls becomes longer and longer. It keeps them interested and the search engines check your website at regular intervals if you feed them new content on a regular basis.

Maintain the quality of your blog posts and make them interesting. Other bloggers will reference your blog content in their own blogs and include a link to your blog post, resulting in what are known as authoritative links or inbound links. This is extremely beneficial to your SEO and will increase traffic to your website.

When you write niche-specific posts with a narrow focus, you have the opportunity to use long-tailed keywords, which are search phrases made up of several words. Blog posts that focus on the benefits of a specific product or meet a specific customer need will generate more traffic from visitors who are interested in those specific aspects of the product you offer, benefiting your optimization.

Your blog posts have long-term optimization benefits that last for weeks and months after you publish a specific blog post without having to redo it.

Advantages for Your Brand

The dropshipping business model is highly competitive, and many competitors take a shortcut by researching what other stores in the same niche are doing and stealing ideas from these stores for their own store design and marketing.

Use your writing skills to highlight features of your own store that set it apart from other stores in your niche, as well as specifics about specific products you offer. Visitors will remember you if you use these subtle reminders in your blog posts, and they will recognise your store as a result of your blogging. A competitor cannot easily use this type of blog post as they would with more generic posts.

Prospective customers consider specialty stores to be those that serve a niche and sell all of the products associated with that niche. They believe that if you specialise, you are an authority in that niche and a responsible seller who understands all of the community's specific issues, needs, and desires. For example, if your niche is fishing and all the related equipment and gadgets, they believe your knowledge and input can be trusted.

Your blog posts allow you to demonstrate to your customers that you are knowledgeable and a member of that niche community. One of the best ways to build your brand is through well-thought-out blog posts.

Advantages of Marketing

It is not difficult to successfully use your blog to promote your business across all social media platforms. The rule is to provide readers with high-quality content rather than generic content that they can find elsewhere. Post links to your blog articles on your social media accounts, then go a step further.

Present the contents of your blog posts in a variety of eye-catching formats that can be used on other platforms. Infographics and product educational videos are two of the most popular formats, and people enjoy sharing them, particularly within a niche community. This broadens your audience and has the potential to bring in new customers.

Improved Customer Relations

People enjoy learning about topics about which they are unfamiliar or want to learn more. What they don't like is being lectured; it makes them feel out of control, as if they're back in school. This is why your blog is so valuable to your company; people feel more at ease being educated through blogs because it is informal and they are not being lectured.

With informative blog articles, you can educate your customers about the industry your niche represents as well as provide general information about your company and products. Instead of directly confronting your customers with a sales pitch, blog to show them that you are upfront and honest, and that you care about their needs and desires.

People prefer reading blog posts to visiting your website's FAQ page. Answer questions on your blog.

A great idea is to write a short series of articles that address the most frequently asked questions customers have about products, service delivery, and other topics.

Your blog posts and comments demonstrate to your store and website visitors that you are approachable and eager to maintain communication between your company and its customers. When visitors leave comments, do some research on them and leave encouraging feedback. You gain insight into your customers' behaviour patterns, allowing you to better plan your marketing strategies.

CHAPTER 13

PERFECT YOUR WEBSITE FOR SELLING

For many people, search engine optimization is a terrifying concept. They immediately consider complications and technology, as well as the money they will need to spend to hire an expert. Yes, SEO can be complicated, but once you grasp the fundamentals, the picture becomes much clearer and everything you need to do makes sense.

Your dropshipping website must be optimised in order for you to be found by search engines. You must have a high search ranking in order to appear high enough when potential customers search for your items. Otherwise, you will not be able to make sales.

Setting up your website for selling and conversions fall under marketing, so it's understandable that many entrepreneurs are perplexed when we talk about optimising your website for selling. The two ideas work in tandem to bring potential customers to your website and keep them there long enough to make a sale.

The most frequently asked question is whether SEO can truly help to increase conversion rates. The answer is unequivocally yes. We will walk you through each step of the process once you understand why your website needs to be optimised.

Make Your Website a Workhorse

Conversion rates across e-commerce websites are currently at 2.5 percent. This means that simply having a great looking website is insufficient. To increase the conversion rate of your website traffic, you must first research your target audience and cater to their needs and desires. Making your website work as hard as possible is one way to increase customer loyalty. With simple site navigation, you can provide your visitors with the best possible customer experience.

This is why you must optimise your website; if your audience cannot find you, there will be no conversions.

Attend to Your Audience's Expectations

You use lead magnets to give your customers what they want, giving them a reason to want your products. When a visitor comes to your website, let's say your niche is outdoor kitchens, they are looking for a new wood burning stove. When a visitor arrives at your website, he is presented with an in-depth blog article outlining the benefits of wood burning stoves and the best models for various situations. This immediately catches his eye. At the end of the article, you entice him to join your email list by offering him a downloadable ebook with decor ideas and information on which models are best suited to various types of outdoor kitchens.

A few days later, you follow up on the lead magnet by offering something like a free consultation with a decor expert in his area. You have a conversion because you met the customer's needs and exceeded his expectations. This scenario applies to whatever your niche products are and whatever incentives are best suited to them.

Optimization is the key to attracting customers to your website, and your efforts to appeal to your site visitors will secure you a new customer.

Website Attraction for a Specific Niche Audience

Your goal and the search engines' goals are the same; the methods used are simply different. You must analyse the behaviour patterns of customers in your specific niche, and Google analyses literally millions of websites using over 200 different ranking factors, but your goals are the same. To provide the best possible experience for your website visitors by presenting them with excellent content and prioritising the contents that provide the most value.

Semantic keywords are the words and phrases used by the person using the search engine to find what he or she is looking for, also known as search intent. When you optimise your website for sales with the goal of increasing conversions, you direct website traffic to buy your products, sign up for your email lists, or join your social media pages.

When you optimise for both your website's goals and SEO at the same time, you create a much better working relationship and interaction between the search engines and your website, which leads to increased customer satisfaction.

Natural Traffic

Businesses spend a lot of money on paid advertising every year to attract visitors when search traffic clicks on one of your sponsored listings or a paid advertisement. Nonetheless, this type of advertising has a conversion rate of less than 2% on average.

While it is true that developing and promoting your website content takes time, effort, and money, the organic traffic you gain through SEO is free. Customers who find your website through organic search have a much higher conversion rate, at over 14 percent.

Investing your time, effort, and money to increase organic traffic to your website takes time, and many people are impatient for instant results. Paid advertising produces short-term results, whereas organic traffic produces long-term results with a much higher conversion rate.

Analyzing Website Data

The first step in the website optimization process is to analyse the data from your website. This allows you to see website visitor behavioural patterns, which will help you decide where to apply and focus your SEO efforts.

Google Search Console is an excellent tool that provides user behaviour reports such as tracking key metrics for your bounce rate, number of sessions, and unique sessions of visitors, and the behaviour reports show you how your site visitors behave while on your website, which pages they visited the most, and which specific pages lead to the best conversion rates.

Keyword Investigation

Search engine optimization has evolved dramatically in the last decade. You can't just pick a few keywords you think are relevant and go with them, write an article or two, and expect to be ranked. It is now a precise science, with numerous factors calculated to achieve the desired first page ranking in search results.

Ubersuggest is a fantastic free keyword search tool for locating keywords related to your niche, niche products, and business. This tool is excellent for locating long-tail keywords that correspond to the user intent of your website's visitors and prospective customers. With Ubersuggest, you can use broad keywords and then filter the keyword results in various ways to get long-tail keywords to target, say, a specific audience within your niche.

There are several tools similar to Ubersuggest, both free and paid for, so try them all until you find one that you feel most at ease with.

Value-added content

In previous chapters, we discussed the importance of providing valuable content and the benefits you receive. This is also true for SEO and search engine rankings.

Run a search for your primary keyword to determine the optimal length of your content for optimization. Examine the top ten SERPs results for that keyword and note the length of those pages. This gives you a good idea of how long the posts you should focus on should be.

This is significant because it informs Google that you are providing a significant amount of information and that people spend a significant amount of time on that specific page, which is beneficial to your search ranking.

On-Page Search Engine Optimization

Maintain a clean and simple on-page optimization strategy. On-page SEO aims to use your website's design, images, and words to help search engines understand it.

Identify and Use a Few Relevant Keywords Strategically

Using a tool like Ubersuggest, find a few of the most relevant keywords that describe the core of your niche or your products. Use the chosen keywords a few times on each page and make sure they flow naturally throughout the content. Cramming keywords and key phrases into each page will not improve your search ranking because search engine algorithms are sophisticated and ignore keyword cramming.

Image Enhancement

Instead of the generic "image.jpg" for image file names and alt tags, find relevant ways to use your keywords for image file names and alt tags. Taking the extra time to properly optimise your images benefits your on-page SEO.

Internal Hyperlinks

Internal links are hyperlinks within a page's content that point to another page on your website that contains relevant information. Internal links spread link equity, also known as link juice in layman's terms, across your website by transferring page authority to another page. So, if you have some pages that don't rank well, you can use an internal link to connect them to a higher-ranking page. Internal links aid in the promotion of pages with lower rankings.

Individual pages cannot be crawled by search engine spiders unless they have internal links pointing to other pages.

Link Explorer is an excellent tool that takes the confusion out of internal linking with several great features and is well worth purchasing if you are unsure how to go about creating internal links.

Optimization for Mobile Devices

The graph below depicts how rapidly mobile devices have become the preferred method of accessing the internet in recent years. As a result, optimising websites for mobile users has become a requirement.

(2019, Perficient Digital)

Google launched the mobile-first index in 2018, so optimising your website for mobile is a must. Otherwise, you risk losing a sizable percentage of conversions from mobile internet users.

Responsive design is the simplest way to make your website mobile friendly. WordPress relieves you of the burden of coding by providing free and premium themes with responsive design built-in.

High-Quality Backlinks

Google considers backlinks to be a sign of your website's credibility, which influences your ranking. Backlinks must come from a reputable website, according to the rule. It does not help your ranking if you have a lot of backlinks but they come from untrustworthy websites. When it comes to earning search engine credibility, quality definitely trumps quantity.

Obtaining high-quality backlinks requires time and effort on your part, as it takes time and effort to cultivate trustworthy backlinks. It is worthwhile because quality backlinks are SEO gold, and with so many ways to obtain backlinks, it can be enjoyable rather than a chore.

Infographics are one of the most popular ways to obtain backlinks. Make eye-catching infographics that people will want to see and share. Guest blogging is another popular way to obtain backlinks. Writing excellent articles for other website blogs not only earns you backlinks, but it also introduces new audiences to your own website and improves your online reputation.

Donating to non-profit organisations is an intriguing way to earn backlinks. Look for websites in your niche that not only accept donations but also link back to websites from which they received donations.

These are just a few methods for obtaining high-quality backlinks; there are numerous others to consider. Be inventive in your search for link-building opportunities that interest you and are relevant to your niche.

Page loading time

Your site's performance, or how quickly your pages load, has a significant impact on SEO and your customer conversion rate. Shoppers are not willing to wait for a slow webpage to load, and nearly half of all visitors to websites with slow loading times will abandon their carts. They abandon the page if it takes more than three seconds to load.

Google added a page speed update to their algorithm in 2018, making it critical to ensure your website has fast page loading as this affects your search page ranking.

Soasta Inc. (2010a)

It is not difficult to solve the slow page speed problem and improve your ranking and conversion rate.

Google's Page Speed Insights is the best app to use to fix this issue. The app provides a detailed breakdown of your website's loading time on mobile devices and desktop computers. The app then gives you step-by-step instructions on how to fix the problems and improve your page loading speed, as well as strategies for reducing server calls, file size, and load speed.

CHAPTER 14

HOW TO GROW YOUR DROPSHIPPING COMPANY

The ability to scale is critical for the success of a dropshipping business. Without growth, your company will stagnate, which is the beginning of the end for any company. Whatever your personal objectives are for your

If you want to become a business mogul or simply have a comfortable and sustainable business, you must scale. The idea of scaling can be intimidating because you will be stepping outside of your comfort zone and taking on more responsibilities. However, if you approach scaling your business step by step and use all of the tools and strategies available, it becomes simple and exciting to watch your company grow.

Scaling is not a one-size-fits-all method of expanding your business. It is very adaptable, and if one method of scaling does not work for your niche, you have a variety of other options to try out and implement those that work best for your specific dropshipping business. That is what makes scaling so successful; you can add as many different options as you want; there are no restrictions.

Are You Prepared?

Premature scaling is a term used in business to describe expanding your business without first laying a solid foundation on which to build your scaling. It is not only new businesses that fall into this trap; even long-established businesses do, and the result is invariably failure.

Before you can be ready to scale, you must complete the following steps in order for your scaling efforts to be successful.

Cash Security Net

2017 (Hackermoon)

Create a cash safety net for your business before scaling to account for any setbacks that may occur during the scaling process. This will allow you to change strategies while scaling and have cash to fall back on if one strategy fails. You won't be able to try more than one strategy to find the perfect product and market fit if you don't have a cash reserve.

Steps in the Right Direction

You must follow the steps from the beginning to the end of the scaling process in the correct order. Starting at the wrong end of your scale will result in a lot more work, wasted money, and missed opportunities.

When you commit to the scaling process, you lose flexibility because you've begun spending money on products, hiring a person or people to help run the business, and advertising.

It is not difficult to avoid all of the problems associated with premature scaling. Spend no money on non-essentials and save all extra cash to allow you to progress without running out of money in the middle of scaling. Once that is in place, you must ensure that you understand exactly what your customers want, that you have all of the ways to reach potential customers, and that you have established strategies and advertising to reach all of your potential customers in the target group of your scaling effort. The final step is to put any products you want to scale or new products you want to add to your business to the test. Scaling must be based on proven test results, not guesses or what people claim are the latest trends or fads. Once you've completed all of the preceding steps, you've eliminated the possibility of premature scaling and are ready to begin scaling your dropshipping business.

Vertical Sizing

Traditional vertical scaling entails adding more products or expanding on the categories in your niche. You also increase your advertising budget for existing ad sets that are performing exceptionally well. In short, you increase your ad spend while not focusing on finding new audiences to target within your niche. This is a good, solid scaling method with a proven track record.

Horizontal Scaling

Scaling horizontally provides you with several options, or combinations of horizontal scaling options, to implement, whichever best fits your business and is the most comfortable to use. Essentially, instead of scaling your existing products upwards, you scale by introducing your products to new audiences – you scale wide.

Start Your Own Business

You duplicate your existing business and online store in order to sell to clients in your niche who speak a different language. If you speak more than one language, you can handle this on your own by simply translating everything on your current website to the target language.

If you do not speak another language, form a partnership with someone who does and split the profits from the new franchise website 50/50 with this person.

Duplicating your business in another language has a greater appeal to people in countries where English is not the official language. Shoppers in Europe, the Balkans, and the Far East prefer to shop online in their native language, and the Euro is their preferred payment currency.

The advantage of duplicating is that you will have a higher conversion rate, but you will also take on a lot more work and be limited in the number of countries you can target in your scaling efforts.

Maintain Your English While Expanding Globally

Scaling globally and keeping everything in English has the disadvantage of losing potential clients who do not want to do business in English and prefer to pay in USD, resulting in a lower conversion rate.

To compensate for this disadvantage, scale globally for countries where English is the official or one of the official languages. This type of global scaling requires far less effort than duplicating your website, freeing up time to focus on other aspects of your business.

Scaling Up Into Neighboring Markets

This is a great way to scale your business by researching the niches that border your own and looking for products in these neighbouring niches that would complement the products you are already selling. Look for products that customers in your niche would be interested in purchasing, and test the response to the new products by offering a few at a time. Your sales statistics will clearly show you which products your niche customers prefer, allowing you to make adjustments to the products you offer from adjacent niches. You can do this type of scaling indefinitely without spending extra money on advertising until you are certain that any neighbouring niche products are viable for permanent inclusion.

Lookalike Audiences on Facebook

Facebook has a segmentation tool that generates lookalike audiences based on your current followers. The tool uses your followers' interests and demographics to create a lookalike audience that you can target. Because the demographics and interests of the new audience closely match those of your current followers, this method of scaling allows for more targeted marketing and identifies groups with a high potential conversion rate.

Facebook searches its massive user base for similarities in order to create a lookalike audience that would not have been discovered without the user data stored within Facebook. This tool works as long as your client group has at least 100 people, but the larger your total, the more effective this tool becomes.

You can build your lookalike audience from your customer lists, website traffic, and fan pages, and you can choose between different types of lookalike audiences.

Demographic Information

You can refine your demographics for the lookalike audience by specifying a specific location, gender, and age group to target your advertising even more precisely.

Choosing an Audience Size

Choose the large audience option to increase the number of people you reach who are similar to your current audience. This will give you a much larger audience, but there will be fewer similarities shared than your fans and current customers.

When you choose a smaller lookalike audience, fewer people will see your ads, but those people will share far more characteristics with your fans and clients.

Facebook's CFO

The campaign budget optimization (CBO) feature was introduced by Facebook in September 2019 to optimise how your advertising budget is distributed. This algorithm now optimises your ad budget across all of your ad sets in real time. It targets the best opportunities separately, optimising them one by one based on what it considers to be the lowest cost per result. Once an opportunity has been exhausted, it moves on to the next best opportunity. It does not account for the amount spent on the previous ad set. The advantage of CBO is that the algorithm targets your top performing ad sets, and you no longer waste money on opportunities that are much less likely to lead to sales and conversions by intelligently optimising your campaign budget to target the ads that perform best and the audiences that respond best.

Customer Match and Google Similar Audiences

Google provides several tools to help you re-engage customers and scale your business.

Customer Match uses data that customers have shared with you, both offline and online, to re-engage them across Display, YouTube, Search, Gmail, and Shopping. This tool can also be used to target other potential clients who are similar to the ones you already have.

Google's Similar Audiences tool works in the same way as Facebook's Lookalike tool. Similar Audiences searches frequently use your marketing lists and first-party data information to target new users who share similar characteristics and interests as your best performing website visitor groups.

Plan and Estimate

For scaling to be successful, it is critical to plan ahead of time. You must perform two specific forecast evaluations in order to plan accurately. To provide you with the most realistic results, it is critical to be as thorough as possible with as much data as possible.

A forecast of customer growth, broken down into categories and broken down by different months, with specifics such as the number of new clients and the estimated number of orders.

An expense forecast along the same lines as the sales growth forecast for what systems you have in place and will require to handle the increased number of orders. Also, what changes will be required to your infrastructure, what technological upgrades will be required, and how much extra manpower will be required to run the business during the scaling period.

Suppliers

Suppliers are an important part of growing your business. You must be able to trust that your suppliers will be able to scale with you and that you will not be dealing with a supplier who is unable to keep up with your increased orders in the middle of your scaling operation. Make certain that your supplier can keep up, particularly if your scaling involves custom products or new products on the market. If you have any doubts about the supplier's ability, it is best to look for a new or backup supplier.

When you begin scaling communication with your suppliers, you include them in the equation. Suppliers are fully aware of the advantages that scaling will bring to their own business. They would prefer that you remain loyal to them, so bargain for the best prices on the products you are scaling. If you have a good working relationship with your suppliers, the majority of them will be willing to negotiate.

Personnel in Support

As your business grows and orders increase, you will require support staff because you will no longer be able to handle the orders coming in, customer queries, and placing orders on your own. No company can afford to have a bad relationship with its customers, especially new customers. You must have a competent person or persons on staff who can assist you in dealing with customer inquiries as well as communicating with and placing orders with your suppliers.

Outsourcing by hiring a virtual assistant or virtual assistants for your specific business requirements is a cost-effective way to have the needed support staff in place. You can train and introduce your virtual assistant to your suppliers without spending money on extras like office space or equipment. This means you can use the funds in your cash reserve for other purposes within your company.

Automation and technology

Automation is at the top of the list for the smooth operation of any dropshipping company, and this is especially true during the scaling process. There simply isn't time to do tasks manually because they are too time consuming, leaving you with little or no time to focus on the numerous extra tasks that must be completed in order to scale successfully.

Automate order fulfilment and auto order tracking are two types of automation to put in place before you start scaling. These to automation options keep orders being placed going and keep customers happy as they can track the progress of their orders. Tracking is especially beneficial when you are dealing with first time customers who may be uncomfortable dealing with a company they do not really know.

Make sure that you integrate as many of your systems as possible to prevent communications problems. The more unintegrated systems you have, the higher the chances are that the systems will not function well together, so prevent problems further along the line by integrating your systems to the greatest extent possible

CHAPTER 15

TO AVOID PITFALLS AND MISTAKES

We purposefully saved this section for last. This is not a doom and gloom chapter; rather, it is your go-to section that you will frequently refer to when problems arise. Everything we discuss here is intended to help you navigate the inevitable pitfalls you will face when starting your own dropshipping business, as well as how to avoid falling into the traps that so many dropshippers before you have.

People do not fail in dropshipping businesses because they are stupid. When you first start out, everyone wants you to succeed, which puts a lot of pressure on you. People make mistakes because they become impatient to succeed and take dangerous shortcuts. The most common mistakes in the success of a dropshipping business occur when you simply do not know what to look for and what to avoid.

The important thing to remember about this chapter is that others have made these mistakes before you, and some have given up or suffered financial losses as a result. They've been there, done that, and you can learn from their experiences. This chapter will assist you in successfully navigating the intricate maze of e-commerce.

Failure to Learn from Mistakes

You are a human being, and you will make mistakes. The number one mistake that entrepreneurs can make is to learn nothing from the mistakes made. Nobody starts out having all the information about dropshipping; you learn as you go along and if you make mistakes, you learn from them. When an issue crops up, you find solutions and ways to avoid making that same mistake again.

When you choose not to learn or make no effort to find out how to correct problems and mistakes, you set your dropshipping business up for failure.

Customers, Audience

When you start your dropshipping business, you need to know what your market. Thinking that having products in the latest trend is going to automatically be successful does not work. You need to know exactly who your target audience is, guessing is a costly mistake. Research is key; you must gather statistical data about your niche audience and get to know everything possible about them.

In Chapter 12, we discussed cross-selling and upselling as market strategies. Not upselling is a mistake many dropshipping companies still making. Get to know your target audience well enough to generate sales from upselling or your profit margin will stay limited. Have a solid upselling plan ready and don't only rely on your front-end products to generate sales. Upselling is far more cost-effective marketing as you do not spend money advertising these products.

To bring in real money for your business, you need value your previous customers. You have already made the connection and a sale, neglecting to keep in contact through your email lists is a huge mistake to make. Do not focus only on getting new customers, staying in touch with your previous customers form a large part of your overall profit margin.

One of the biggest mistakes newbies make is to try to take on the whole world when they start their dropshipping business. You need to learn to walk before you can run, so focus on your target audience within the USA. Get to know your target audience in the USA where you have a vast niche audience with fast and trustworthy shipping. Once you have established your USA market and gained experience, you can think of going global.

Website

Two mistakes that pop up regularly regarding the dropshipping business store and website are the website structure and product descriptions and names that are badly edited.

Stores and websites that are not neatly and logically set up confuse prospective customers and they soon leave. Not everyone is skilled in coding and HTML, nor is a solution readily available.

Shopify has all of the apps and plugins needed to set up a functional store, and the Woocommerce plugin on the WordPress system is available for more experienced entrepreneurs.

Dropshipping companies that use online platforms like Alibaba and Aliexpress and plugins to import products to their store and website are unaware that product names and descriptions must be edited. The product descriptions and names are irrelevant to your own dropshipping business; they must be edited to focus your target audience.

SEO

Despite all of the information available about search engine optimization and the critical role it plays in a business's online visibility and conversion rate, this is still a huge problem. Any aspect of SEO that is overlooked will have a long-term negative impact on your business. If you don't think you can do it alone, use one of the many apps and plugins available.

Niche

The two most common niche mistakes are choosing a niche without conducting extensive research into that niche and choosing a niche that is too broad. When you don't do any research, you're more likely to pick the wrong niche after you've set up and branded your store. This is a costly error because you must then restart from scratch. When you can't use precise and focused keywords, choosing a too broad niche is disastrous for marketing, promotions, and SEO.

Brand Recognition

Brand visibility is just as important for your dropshipping business as for any other retail company. It is a mistake to not keep your brand as visible as possible at every opportunity. Custom external packaging, a thank you note after delivery, and sending out customer satisfaction surveys are simple, yet effective, ways to keep your brand visible.

Customer Support

Poor customer service destroys your business. Customers and potential customers must be prioritised, and failing to respond quickly and efficiently to customer complaints, queries, and questions marks your company as one to avoid, particularly on social media.

Unrealistic Predictions

Many startup businesses have failed because they entered dropshipping with the unrealistic expectation of making easy money with little or no effort. Enter the market with your eyes wide open. The recipe for success is to know how to market your products, who your target audience is, how to compete with the many competitors out there, and to be willing to put in the effort.

A common mistake is to believe that once you've set up your online store and created a website, that's all you have to do to earn a passive income. If you don't do anything, nothing will happen.

If you don't see immediate success or if a strategy fails, you should give up. There is no such thing as instant success or failure in business; it takes perseverance and time to succeed.

Inability to accept negative feedback from customers on social media platforms, your store, and your website. Negative feedback is not a personal attack; every business receives negative feedback; this does not imply that your business is a failure. Deal with the negative feedback, come up with solutions, and move on.

Goods with a Patent

Many dropshipping businesses have failed because they sold trademarked products. The trademark laws in the USA and the EU are very strict and harsley enforced, it is simply not worth it to lose everything you worked for plus the chance of being sued.

Suppliers

Overdependence on a single supplier occurs when an entrepreneur is comfortable with a supplier who has consistently provided good service. Anything can happen, such as stock shortages, unexpected massive price increases, or the supplier receiving an influx of orders and being unable to fulfil them all. Even if your niche is narrowly focused, it is always a good idea to have a backup supplier.

Marketing

The most common reason dropshipping companies employ poor marketing strategies is that they do not understand their niche customers well enough. As a result, their marketing is promoted to everyone rather than narrowly targeting their niche customers.

Another blunder is that they promote their products at random rather than researching the specific channels where the majority of their customers are active. The results of random marketing are mediocre at best, with very low returns.

Legal Obligations and Taxes

Legal liabilities are a stumbling block for many startups, and many try to avoid them. To avoid legal liabilities, register your dropshipping business as a corporation. Once you have legally registered your company, the company, not you personally, is liable for all agreements, contracts, and business transactions.

Sales tax is perplexing and causes numerous errors. Shopify and Woocommerce platforms help sellers who open shops on their platforms by providing settings that automatically collect sales taxes on products.

Order Processing

It is easy to fall into the trap of manually fulfilling orders when starting a business, and many people do. This works well in the beginning, but as the business grows, they are unable to keep up. Use an app like Oberlo to automate your order fulfilment and save yourself a lot of time.

When people shop online, they make mistakes, such as changing their minds about which product they want or deciding to cancel an order. It is your responsibility to ensure that this process is handled correctly and professionally in order to ensure customer satisfaction. Ensure that your supplier confirms any changes with you and then confirms with the customer that the changes were made, or the correct refunds will be applied.

CONCLUSION

You now have everything you need to get started with your dropshipping business. Begin small and aim high. You know what to look out for and what to avoid. Many people have a morbid desire to give entrepreneurs unsolicited advice by telling horror stories of failure and squandering money by starting a dropshipping business. Don't pay attention to them.

Building a dropshipping business takes time; it does not happen overnight. When your biggest investment is yourself, success will follow. Your efforts, your time, your tenacity, and your determination to succeed.

It is natural to feel overwhelmed when you first begin. But keep in mind that every step you take is a step forward. The most difficult aspect of running a dropshipping business is getting started. It makes no difference if you are unsure about something; most people are simply terrified of starting a business.

Start off on the right foot, and you've already won half the battle. Think carefully and don't rush into things, only to have to go back and correct your mistakes. Use every tool at your disposal to take advantage of all the features of the dropshipping software that is appropriate for your niche.

Despite the fact that many people claim it is not a sustainable business model, the dropshipping business model is extremely popular. Remember, Jeff Bezos began in a tiny office with computer wires everywhere and a handwritten banner with his company name on the wall, and Bill Gates began in his garage.